SEA ANGLING FROM THE SHORE

SEA ANGLING FROM THE SHORE

Ray Forsberg

Line illustrations by Baz East

DAVID & CHARLES
Newton Abbot   London   North Pomfret (Vt)

British Library Cataloguing in Publication Data

Forsberg, Ray
  Sea angling from the shore.
  1. Saltwater fishing
  I. Title
  799.1'6   SH457

  ISBN 0 7153 8147 4

Photoset by Typesetters (Birmingham) Limited
and printed in Great Britain
by Redwood Burn Limited, Trowbridge, Wilts
for David & Charles (Publishers) Limited
Brunel House Newton Abbot Devon

Published in the United States of America
by David & Charles Inc
North Pomfret Vermont 05053 USA

Contents

Introduction

In these days of increased leisure time, some of it enforced by employment problems, redundancies and early retirements, the exhilarating sport of sea angling, and in particular fishing from the shoreline, is steadily booming. All around this island home of ours, there are waters to be fished, quite free of charge, all the year round. The tackle which comprises an initial angling outfit is not prohibitively expensive when compared with other outdoor pursuits, and bait can be obtained for the taking once a few simple tools and a little littoral zone know-how have been acquired.

After almost fifty years of continuous sea angling, I have tried to concentrate within the covers of this book all the shore lore, tackle tips, bait-digging wrinkles, fish-catching techniques and safety precautions I have amassed in that time. The sea and its mysteries will never fail to fascinate me. Likewise, the glorious uncertainty of what may become attached to the end of my line is always exciting. The tideline in all its many moods throughout the year brings great variety to my angling. Perhaps when you come to the end of these pages, you will discover that I have generated within you a little of my enthusiasm for all things piscatorial. I sincerely hope so.

Think deeply about your fishing. Treasure the marine environment and do all in your power to protect it from being defiled. It is a precious heritage which we must try to hand over to our offspring in an unspoiled state so that they can enjoy it as much as we have done.

RAY FORSBERG

1
Shorefishing Around Our Coastline

The modern trend on the British angling scene towards saltwater fishing, currently termed by the sport fishing fraternity as 'The swing to the sea', has been brought about, almost certainly, by the surfeit of frustrating restrictions which hamper the other two branches of the sport, commonly known as game (salmon and trout) and coarse (freshwater) fishing. In a world fraught with petty annoyances of all kinds, those magical words 'The sea is free' are a breath of fresh air to the longsuffering coarse or game fisherman whose wallet is stuffed to bursting point with licences, permits, club cards, Angling Association booklets, fishery rules and written reminders outlining forbidden methods or bait bans.

Inland, away from the shoreline, every river, canal, stream, reservoir, lake, duckpond or diminutive puddle, seems to be controlled and jealously guarded by someone who has proudly erected a NO FISHING or PRIVATE ANGLING sign. Is it any wonder that a newcomer with piscatorial inclinations takes one apprehensive glance at all those inhibiting notices and decides that this section of the angling scene is definitely not for him?

Disenchanted with all the restrictions which thwart the coarse or game angler, the prospective amateur takes himself off to the coast—buying a set of tackle on the way—and joyfully walks down to the shoreline to cast out his bait, and his cares, into the wide blue yonder. He is secure in the knowledge that there are no bailiffs, close-season bans, bait or method restrictions to mar his pleasure. Wherever he chooses to angle in the sea (except for just a few private piers, yacht marinas, harbours and estuaries) the fish are there for the catching, and he is not liable to fall foul of the law in availing himself of such a gloriously free privilege. There is the added bonus that he can do it all the year round, day or night.

Before the advent of rod and line fishing, sea angling was practised on a much smaller scale, with strong handlines, primarily as a means of procuring cheap food rather than as a sporting pastime. All its exponents could be called 'frying pan fishermen'. But modern use of highly sophisticated tackle and angling methods has brought about a vastly different situation from that which existed at the beginning of the century.

Today there are about two million sea anglers in this country, the majority of whom are shore fishing devotees. They can be roughly divided into four categories. By far the greatest number are 'pan fishermen' pure and simple; if it swims close to the shore and is edible, then that is the fish which is their target. This group of anglers usually live right on, or quite near to, the coast, so that they can put in long, regular fishing sessions all the year round. They are generally resourceful people who make up a lot of their own tackle and, of course, they study the shoreline carefully so that they can provide all their own bait. The 'pan fishermen' are usually able to keep the freezer regularly topped-up with fresh fish fillets throughout the year, which represents a weekly saving of quite a few pounds.

I shall call the second category of shore anglers 'specimen hunters' as they closely resemble their counterparts in the coarse fishing world. These are the sea fishermen who spend their time pursuing either the biggest fish of a distinct selection of species, or, perhaps, the monsters of a single species. The bass addicts immediately spring to mind. Whereas the 'pan fishermen' enjoy the company of other anglers and often angle together in small groups the sea 'specimen hunters' are usually very much lone-wolf performers.

When seeking big fish, which may be very thin over the shoreline, it is a great asset to have the only bait in the water. By that piscatorial logic, if a real rodbender comes along there will be only one angler in line to catch it. Normal sociable fishing hours have absolutely no meaning to 'specimen hunters'. The only thing that matters is that the fish are there to be caught. Tides and weather conditions are the saltwater imponderables which control the lives of big fish enthusiasts. Mealtimes, normal bed times and even festive occasions like Christmas Day have no special significance for them. If the bait is to hand and the weather and the tide are right, then you will find them with rod in hand, concentrating hard on their fishing and thoroughly enjoying themselves speculating just how big the fish may be when that vital bite comes.

In considering the third category of shore anglers, we are moving towards the more gregarious type of person who loves good cheerful angling company. I am referring, of course, to the 'sea fishing festival angler'. All around the coastline of the British Isles, particularly in the holiday months from May to September, both boat and shore fishing festivals are run at many seaside resorts for the entertainment of the visitors and also to attract custom, which is vital to the local business people. This is where the 'festival shore fisher' comes onto the scene. Some I know take their annual holidays at the same resort each year and have never missed a fishing festival for perhaps twenty or thirty years. Quite often this is the only occasion when they wet a line in the whole year. Once the holiday is over, the tackle goes back into a dark corner of the garage until next summer. However, for the socially minded angler, festival fishing can certainly be an attractive way of spending a holiday – fishing all day, wining and dining at night – and with the added bonus of perhaps a colour television or an automatic washing machine at the end of the week when the aggregate weight totals or heaviest fish figures are worked out.

Finally, we have the 'sea match angler'. A few members of this august and affluent body can be given the 'professional' tag, as they seem to follow occupations which play second fiddle to their fishing. These are the real glamour boys or 'stars' of the sea shore-

11

fishing scene. Practically every sea shore match which is held on our coastline is won by one of a select band of anglers who travel around the country competing for substantial cash prizes or goods of high value which can easily be converted into cash. As one very successful sea match angling friend of mine remarked: 'Being unable to watch two colour TV sets at once, I naturally turned the second I won into a wad of crackling fivers.'

To attain the success which they quite rightly deserve, the top-class shore match anglers need to be really expert in every phase of the angling game. Their tackle handling and casting must be polished and superb; so far as shore lore is concerned, they must have a wide knowledge of all types of coastline and fish movements; and they must be able to provide themselves with the best of bait at all times of the year. In addition, they must possess a sixth sense which tells them exactly what terminal tackle, bait and location will produce fish in the most difficult angling conditions imaginable – a hot, sunny day on a crowded beach or pier.

This country is blessed with such a wide variety of shorelines that the sea angler who likes different terrain to test his skill need never be at a loss for somewhere new and challenging to fish. For ease of reference, natural shorecasting venues can be grouped into five loose categories.

Apart from man-made structures, such as harbour walls, groynes, piers and jetties, I would say that fairly flat, sandy beaches easily head the list of popular shorecasting spots, although such venues do not necessarily produce the best catches of fish. The reason they are usually so crowded with anglers is that they are most accessible for car parking, they can be fished with relatively light tackle without a great number of terminal rigs being lost and, of prime importance, they are safe places for inexperienced anglers to begin their fishing careers.

Rocky shorelines with steep cliffs, where the sea is quite deep and carpeted with thick weed tangles, are somewhat formidable fishing stations which naturally attract only the most experienced, venturesome and active sea anglers. These places invariably have a good head of resident fish shoals in attendance, as they are impossible to trawl and commercial fishermen give them a wide berth. In some areas, the currents and tide rips are so dangerous around rocky headlands that it would be extremely foolhardy to venture near them in any kind of small boat. Therefore the shorecasting sea angler has a rare chance to cast his tackle into what amounts to completely untapped, virgin territory where the fish-producing potential may be nothing short of phenomenal.

One other type of deepwater venue is the steep-to bank of shingle, where the shoreline falls away sharply to give a good depth of water just a few feet from the edge. Two famous shorecasting venues in this category are the Chesil (Dorset) and Dungeness (Kent) shorelines. These are very popular winter cod fishing spots which attract sea anglers in their hundreds when they are producing good bags of fish.

Estuarial mudflats, which are low lying with many creeks and gullies intersecting them, are often wonderful fish-producing areas and they may also have prolific bait beds and gathering areas. They can also be extremely dangerous places for the inexperienced angler to venture upon unless he has previously made a thorough investigation of their geographical location and the state of the tides, and familiarised himself with all the surrounding landmarks.

Finally, there is the mixed rock outcrop, sand, shingle and mud-patch type of shoreline, much loved by bait gatherers and big bass exponents. The sea anglers who live in the South of England refer to this kind of shoreline as 'graunchy' ground.

Because the coastline of the British Isles stretches for well over 7,000 miles, and that of England alone measures (without indentations) in the region of 1,500 miles, all composed of varying seascapes ranging from flat sand to towering cliffs, sheer rock faces to shingle beaches, mudflats to marshes, a whole range of different tackle set-ups, methods and baits has evolved over the years to deal effectively with every fishing situation. In some areas, particularly around exposed, rocky headlands, on open

13

beaches and in estuary mouths where very powerful tides flow, the strength of the line and the amount of weight used to hold the terminal tackle firm on the bottom need to be far in excess of that required just for the operation of catching the fish. The type of tackle used is invariably dictated by the fishing conditions encountered, rather than by the weight, size or power of the fish which are to be caught. Likewise, over very snaggy ground consisting of rocks with great beds of tackle-hungry kelp, it would be quite fatal from the point of view of tackle loss to adopt the same gear and methods as are used over gently sloping sandy beaches with never a stone in sight. In these situations the gentle tide run will allow a mere 2oz of lead to be used. Inside some harbours, estuaries, or rivermouths and along some kinds of shoreline where there is very little tidal flow, the very lightest of coarse fishing tackle can be used when the fish to be caught are not expected to be particularly large or powerful.

Another important aspect is the casting distance factor, which dictates not only the strength of line used, but also the length and power of the rod employed, and the size and pattern of weight chosen. The most obvious example is the kind of tackle employed on open surf beaches for winter cod fishing, where generally the power of the rod and the strength of the line used would be quite sufficient to land a shark in the 100lb region. However, since the angler will need to cast his baited hook out to at least 80 yards, and more often in the region of 100 to 120 yards, requiring a 5 or 6oz sinker, the rest of the gear – both rod and line – need to be scaled up in both performance and strength to enable them to propel the weight to the distance required to get among the feeding fish.

On the rocky coastline of my native Yorkshire a seemingly crazy set of very strong tackle has been developed over the years. It causes much amusement to those anglers who do not fully understand the diabolically snaggy conditions on some of the shorefishing marks. A very stiff and powerful 9–11ft rod (nowadays in hollow fibre glass, but formerly consisting of solid greenheart or built cane) is used in conjunction with an

14

unwieldy looking 'cart wheel' centrepin reel and nylon monofilament line in the region of 40 to perhaps even 70lb breaking strain. As further evidence of our apparent madness, we Yorkshire anglers use great spoon-shaped lead weights up to the 8oz mark and what is called a 'rotten bottom'–a lead attachment link with a lower breaking strain. This makes for an easy break-out which leaves the lead in the rocks, without the loss of any other item of the terminal tackle or the reel line when the gear becomes snagged. Note I have written 'when' the gear becomes snagged and not 'if', because it is a dead certainty that it will, and at some venues at every three or four casts.

The high cost of shop-bought lead weights would soon see us calling in the Official Receiver, so we have devised a cheaper way to solve the lost sinker problem. We make them ourselves by casting them, literally by the dozen, from old lead water pipes in a sandbox mould. The shape is pressed out in the mould using a large tablespoon. The idea of the spoon-shaped lead has been strongly criticised by many anglers who have no knowledge of rock and kelp fishing marks. Although the spoon-shaped flat lead is quite unsuitable for long casting, as it is aerodynamically the wrong shape to flight easily and truly through the air, it has one great redeeming feature. When being reeled in at a fast speed, it rises up from the sea bed and 'planes' above the rocks and weed, keeping itself and the trailing hook clear of snags.

Where rocky gullies and weed-festooned boulders predominate in which the rock-loving wrasses are sought, heavy float tackle is the only type of terminal equipment which will effectively cut tackle losses to a minimum. The technique which is most successful for this difficult ground is to cast the baited float tackle right into the surging surf quite close to the barnacle-covered rock ledges or 'tables'. A fairly long rod is needed to keep the line clear of the rocks when operating the tackle and particularly when playing and landing the fish. The bait is set at a precise distance beneath the float where it will be suspended just above the rocks and weed. This will be low enough to attract the attention of fish browsing around for edible marine creatures on

15

the bottom, but sufficiently high to avoid snags. Large, easily seen, specially designed saltwater floats are also used from piers, harbour walls and rocky promontories as a means of carrying float tackle on a tiderun out beyond casting range to where fish may be shoaling and feeding.

Two often bewildering factors which directly affect all sea anglers, and particularly those who cast from the shoreline, are the geographical distribution and seasonal migratory habits of their quarry. At certain times of the year, some species move very close inshore either to feed on other lesser fish or to follow the dictates of their spawning or breeding instincts. Conversely, other fish move out into deeper water either to escape the rapid cooling of the shallows as winter approaches or to travel to their breeding grounds in the deeps.

One fish which dominates the shorecasting scene around Britain's coastline, and causes an army of hardy anglers to spend winter nights in the dark on freezing beaches, is the cod. So far as the boat angler is concerned, cod are available in deep offshore water all round the British Isles throughout the year. They are particularly prolific over wrecks lying in deep water, and around oil rigs and offshore installations where all forms of commercial fishing and even rod and line angling are strictly forbidden.

It is generally acknowledged that the shoals of cod and codling (fish up to 5lb in weight) can be expected to move inshore within casting range from about October or November until early springtime. Their distribution is limited roughly to the East coast of Scotland, the North Sea coast of England and the English Channel along the South coast, thinning out towards Cornwall. The lowering of inshore water temperatures, coupled with strong north-easterly gales that churn up the sea bed and dislodge from their hiding places many marine food items, plus the presence close inshore of shoals of small fish which provide a living larder, are the natural occurrences which cause the cod to move shorewards *en masse*.

Water temperature is the vital key to the movements of fish in the sea. Each species has a range of warmth or coldness to which

Typical wrasse country near Land's End

By using selected blanks an individually styled, custom-made rod can be built

A short handled beachcaster makes the ideal pier fishing rod, as it will rest at just the right angle on the average pier handrail

The 'Leeds' 5in 'trotting reel' is ideal for light tackle mullet fishing with a float. Note that the line comes off the top of the reel. This allows an easy flow of line through the rod rings so that the float can pull off the line from the very free running reel

it is best suited. Some fish have a much wider temperature range tolerance than others and they can stray far from their natural habitat without suffering any ill effects. The arctic winter of 1962/3, when the sea froze in some areas around the coast, produced a rapid sea temperature change and enormous numbers of conger eels were washed up dead on the beaches. They had been caught close inshore by the freezing sea temperature and had perished from the intense cold before they could swim out into deeper warmer water. Incidentally it was the same winter which wiped out whole colonies of wrasse around the Cornish coastline and also killed off thousands of lobsters, crabs, shellfish such as razorfish, and whole areas of prolific lugworm beds.

At the turn of the century, a time within living memory for quite a number of people, there were prolific shoals of edible fish in all the seas and oceans of the world. Around the British coast the sea teemed with the most choice varieties of table fish imaginable. In the North Sea, for instance, on the once famous Dogger Bank, there was such a concentration of cod and haddock that it was quite unnecessary for fishing boats to go any further afield to fill their holds. Off Whitby, in North Yorkshire, there was an area (now completely barren) called the Silver Pits which produced prime plaice and the much sought after soles—by the ton.

Then the era of the steam trawler dawned and, from then on, the seas were raped and plundered almost to the point of extinction for some species. Put bluntly, trawling is a method of fishing which should have been outlawed on a worldwide scale from the day someone first conceived the idea. Ecologically it is a marine disaster. It is the most wasteful and destructive method of fishing ever evolved. Basically it consists of dragging an enormously heavy and cumbersome net bag, armed with heavy metal bobbins, chains, otter boards and floats, right through the middle of the flat, sandy bottomed fish breeding grounds. This net disturbs everything in its wake, taking immature fish with the bigger ones and compressing them all into a writhing mass as it is heaved to the surface and winched aboard the trawler, sideways

19

in the older models and stern first in the newer ones.

The sad story of commercial fishing is made even worse, so far as the conservation of fish stocks is concerned, by the fact that over the decades it has been criminally wasteful of good nutritious food. At the height of its success, the trawling industry was taking from the seas such enormous tonnages of prime fish that the market was continually flooded with embarrassingly large amounts. Rather than limit the catch quotas and regulate them to match the amount required for human consumption, the fishing was allowed to carry on completely unchecked. A price was fixed below which fish for eating could not be sold, and the huge residue was either turned into fish manure, pet food and animal feeding stuffs or, at times, dumped back into the sea so that the price would remain high and stable.

Fortunately, the days of trawling are now drawing to a close. Dwindling fish stocks on the high seas make it no longer a viable commercial proposition for the big trawler fleets to put to sea. The cost of their operations in times of galloping inflation has finally outstripped the market value of the fish they can catch, even though its price has risen astronomically. In sheer desperation, the world's trawler fleets have recently attempted to solve their financial problems by switching over to sprat and mackerel fishing, mostly off the Cornish coast – much to the anger of the small-time mackerel and sprat fishermen in that area, who for years have relied upon sprats, pilchards and mackerel for their livelihood.

Finally, to complete the whole chaotic picture, the high price of fish has inspired nearly every small boat operator in the country, both professional and spare-time 'cowboy' alike, to jump on the fish-catching bandwagon and make, as the Americans would term it, a 'fast buck' before the fish finally run out.

Amidst all this gloom and money grabbing, where does the rod and line angler stand? Happily, in quite a good position, provided he is prepared, within the next few years, to voice his opinions loudly, and to band together with anyone interested in the conservation of fish stocks and the preservation of our national heritage of life on an island surrounded by seas filled with fish, rather than an empty nothingness. Once trawling has died a natural death, and worldwide fishery controls have been introduced, with marine National Park areas designated and patrolled by fast fishery protection vessels, prolific fish shoals will once more be found all around the coastline as they were in my boyhood days – a mere fifty years ago.

The price of success for all sea anglers is eternal vigilance. The lawmakers, politicians and those in high places who control our destiny must be firmly pointed in the direction of control and conservation and not allowed to stray from it. Gill netting with monofilament 'mist' nets must immediately be stopped. The minimum takeable fish-size limits should be greatly increased to preserve the dwindling stocks of slow-growing fish like the bass which now face total extinction on the famous Eddystone reef shoaling ground. Sea angling sport fishermen take their fish catches in pounds and sometimes (when they are fortunate) stones, whereas the commercial operators weigh their catches by the hundredweight and often the ton. Do not be misled by the netsman who brings forth the hoary old chestnut 'It is our living – but you only catch fish for fun'. If that sentiment is expressed and applied much longer, there will finally be nothing left for anyone – professional and sport fisherman alike.

2
The Modern Tackle Market

In order to be completely truthful, I may well have appeared to take a somewhat pessimistic and jaundiced view of the fish stocks situation around our coastline. I will now disperse the gloom, however, by making an in-depth appraisal of the modern fishing tackle manufacturing industry, and the retail trade outlets that distribute it to the angler. Both sectors are highly organised and very efficient so far as distribution and after-sales service are concerned. They are also cosmopolitan; many different countries specialise in supplying specific items of tackle which no one else seems to be able to match for performance, design or reliability.

My early boyhood sea angling days, before World War II, were spent casting from a dock wall with a short, stout greenheart 'pole', 6ft long. This was used in conjunction with a 7in wooden Scarborough reel loaded with 'cuttyhunk' flax line, a home-cast spoon-shaped lead, and hooks tied to manufactured 'gut', which was so springy and wire-like when dry that it needed soaking for several hours before any knots could be tied in it. What primitive equipment this was when compared to the highly sophisticated outfits available today. Those cumbersome, unbending wooden 'sea rods' had great heavy porcelain-lined rings whipped to them, which immediately shattered if the rod blew over onto a hard surface. The twisted flax line was unpredictable in both performance and durability. It had to be carefully washed in fresh water after each outing and then loosely coiled around a chair back to dry off. Otherwise it rotted rapidly and caused some very dangerous situations when the 8oz spoon lead was being propelled seawards. On such occasions, a lethal set of terminal tackle, armed with several hooks, would whizz along at head level just above the line of apprehensive anglers (all crouching low) to shatter, with a deafening crash, one of the Dock Master's office windows. Such a happening usually terminated all angling activity on that part of the foreshore for several months, until the hastily erected ANGLING PRO-HIBITED signs were either pulled or blown down.

Without a doubt, two of the greatest scientific discoveries to revolutionise all angling have been synthetic lines and hollow glass (and latterly carbon fibre) rods. These technological miracles, coupled with a recent swing towards all items of fishing tackle being available as DIY kits or separate parts, have given the modern angler undreamed-of freedom in his choice of individually designed, custom-built tackle.

In these enlightened times, when the best made-up tackle and also separate component parts are being imported from suppliers all over the world, it is easily possible to find an angler standing on the beach fishing with a custom-built outfit that he has carefully selected and made up from parts manufactured in several different countries. The 'blanks' from which the rod was made could be of American origin; the rings Japanese; the reel fitting British. The multiplier reel is likely to be Swedish, and the monofilament line German. The swivels on the terminal tackle might be American and the hooks Norwegian. These hybrid outfits are a far cry from the days when there were only three rod types available in the average tackle shop to cater for both coarse and sea fishing. These rods were for roach, pike or sea angling, and were all made up by small British manufacturers and uninterestingly stereotyped in construction, design and finish. The angler's choice was on a par with that offered by Henry Ford to car buyers: you could have any colour you fancied – so long as it was black!

To anyone contemplating the shorecasting scene and thinking of taking up the sport, the choice of what initial outfit to buy must be absolutely bewildering. However, with a little patience and some intelligent forethought, the difficulties can all be

23

surmounted quite easily. I recommend that you first procure as many fishing tackle catalogues from as many different sources as possible. These can be obtained by post or from tackle shops. A glance through the advertising columns of the two weekly angling newspapers, *Angler's Mail* and *Angling Times*, or the three monthly magazines, *Sea Angler*, *Sea Angling Monthly* and *Rod & Line*, will rapidly put the prospective tackle catalogue hunter on the right track. Once these vital catalogues have been obtained and scanned from cover to cover, it is then a quite simple task to pay a few visits to the shoreline to pick the brains of the anglers fishing there. This also provides an opportunity to watch closely and to note how and what they are using in the way of fishing gear. Your local sea angling club will also be glad to provide advice on suitable tackle for the area you intend to fish.

A quick flip through a comprehensive tackle catalogue (which may contain anything up to 300 pages) will reveal that although your local fishing tackle dealer may carry a fairly large stock of items in general demand he just does not have the shelf space nor the working capital to keep a large range of highly specialised items. The moulds for making leads (both freshwater and sea designs) are a typical example. Generally a small tackle dealer will carry only half a dozen different types of the pattern most used in his particular area, whereas a firm specialising in lead casting moulds will put out a small booklet on casting moulds alone, and this is likely to incorporate every type with both freshwater and saltwater examples illustrated.

Let us consider that most vital item of tackle, the hook, as this is the angler's direct link with what he has on the other end of the line. Some anglers are particular, almost to the point of being fanatical, about the quality of the hooks they use. If they cannot obtain exactly what they require their confidence suffers and they fish badly, without that essential optimism which is the secret of making a good catch. The world famous firm of Mustad in Norway fully realise that anglers all have their individual preferences, and to cater for them they produce a staggering 60,000 different types of hook.

Before the introduction of nylon monofilament line tanned brown sea-fishing line and the famous 'cuttyhunk' twisted flax line were the two most popular kinds used. They were sold in different thicknesses rather than a stated breaking strain and they came to the angler in hanks or on wooden spools, the usual quantity being 100 yards. How different the situation is today. Now 'bulk spools' of nylon line are all the rage and are very convenient and economical. They can be bought by weight of line on the spool, in all different breaking strains suitable for sea angling. Starting at 2oz for the smallest, usually in the lower breaking strains 2 to 12lb which are suitable for float fishing and light shorecasting, they range through 4oz, 8oz and 1lb spools in breaking strains of 15 to 40lb and above. In the very lightest range of 2oz spools those in the 2lb bracket carry a length of about 4,000 yards; a 4oz spool of 15lb carries 900 yards. The great advantage of having a bulk spool of nylon line in your tackle bag is that, should you suffer a disaster, either with a 'bird's nest' overrun on a multiplier reel which leaves your line in an almighty tangle, or by becoming snagged or losing a fish which takes with it most of your reel line, it is possible to load up your reel again to full capacity with new line and carry on fishing almost without delay.

Since the great DIY revolution began, the fishing tackle trade, both wholesale and retail, has made every attempt to capture the attention of the angler who wishes to have a custom-made, personalised item of tackle at a rock-bottom, bargain price. Rods particularly lend themselves admirably to the DIY approach, and they can be purchased in various stages of completion. Some need only the rings to be whipped on and the finishing coats of varnish applied, and are suited to the rank amateur rod builder. Others are designed for the accomplished angler who is capable of taking a set of rod 'blanks', rings, reel fitting, handle material, and the whipping thread, varnish etc, and transforming the lot into a finished rod of a standard comparable to the best commercially made product. By making such a fishing rod, at about half or two thirds of the retail cost of the ready-made version, the circumspect angler can also have it highly personalised so far as performance and finish are concerned.

Two important developments in the fishing tackle market which have simplified the task of rod building are the spigot ferrule and Hardloy rings, which are marketed under the trade name Fuji. The old bugbear of ferrule fitting was a job which many amateur rod builders shied away from. The metal ferrules had to be fitted to the rod in exactly the right position – male and female – in order that they would be a perfect fit and function properly. Glueing them into position on the rod 'blanks' was a tricky business because they were apt to 'creep' during the setting process and end up firmly fixed in the wrong positions. This was truly a disaster if they had been stuck with one of the modern adhesives whose makers boast that a permanent bond is made.

Converse to the way in which traditional ferrules functioned, with the female being on the lower section of the rod and the male on the top piece, the spigot ferrule is an integral part of the rod. It is made by glueing a separate piece of glass to protrude from the lower joint so that the upper section fits neatly and tightly over it. By dispensing completely with metal ferrules, which added to the weight of the rod and produced a definite stiffening effect, modern rod designers have taken an enormous step forward in efficiency and performance. Anyone who has been caught in a torrential downpour outside his car at packing-up time and been forced to struggle with a rod fitted with metal ferrules which had become firmly locked as if in a loving embrace will fully realise the importance of the glass spigot ferrule. It very rarely gives any trouble if kept well lubricated with a small cake of paraffin wax, which is gently rubbed on the spigot at regular intervals.

My praise for the modern rod rings is long and loud. Before they came to us (by courtesy of the space research programme) all rings, without exception, were prone to breakage and grooving. The life of an average set on a rod used for beach-casting was about two years, if it was in continual use. Rings with hard ceramic centres could be obtained, which lasted somewhat longer; but they had one grave drawback. They were very heavy and clumsy and were apt to spoil the 'action' of the rod by overloading the tip section, causing it to give a casting action that was not the one intended by the rod designer.

The modern rod rings are wonderful and I have been unable to find a single fault with them. The centres are diamond hard and, as the makers so rightly claim, even a file will not groove them. In addition, they are encased in a shock-absorbing ring made of plastic, which incidentally is coloured green and is luminous. Although rather expensive, Fuji rings prove a sound buy in the long run. They can be whipped onto a rod which gets a great deal of casting use and completely forgotten. With metal rings it is necessary to examine them with a jeweller's eye glass at regular intervals for grooving, which is not always detectable to the naked eye.

If the world of tackle manufacturing and retailing can be said to be highly efficient, the bait market is a totally different proposition. The production and retailing of good tackle is a design and manufacturing process which is completely under the control of us humans. The obtaining of bait, in regular supplies, is governed by a number of natural imponderables which are quite unpredictable. Often the worth of a good tackle dealer can be measured by the effort he puts into supplying his customers with first-class bait. Without a doubt the supply of bait in the right quantity and quality is always an immense headache to the tackle supplier. For this reason some establishments by-pass the bait service altogether. They find themselves unable to live with the problems of unreliable sandworm diggers, refrigeration failures, customers who order and fail to collect, and that ulcer-producing situation when the shop is packed to capacity late on Saturday nights (especially in winter when the cod are in) and the bait diggers are still down on the tideline valiantly and frantically digging in an attempt to fulfil all orders.

One outsize worry for all bait suppliers is the eternal insecurity of the lugworm situation. Lugworms are the mainstay of shore anglers, but the bait position from digger to dealer, and dealer to angler, never reaches the happy state of supply meeting demand. During the hottest summer weather, when the cod are not inshore, there seem to be plenty of lugworms, which no one wants. But once the weather turns cold, the sea roughs up and cod are being taken on all the beaches, then it is necessary to order your bait and pay for it in advance, otherwise you will not stand the ghost of a chance of getting it.

'Short tides' and bad weather are the arch-enemies of bait diggers everywhere, and any thrifty angler who decides to dig or collect his own bait will soon be well acquainted with these annoying problems. Neap tides, which occur every fortnight and last about a week, are those which do not come far up the shoreline or recede a great way down again. The bait diggers cannot therefore get well down the shoreline to the most productive digging grounds where the worms can be dug thick and fast. Also, during the winter months the darkness factor stymies a lot of good digging time. When the low-water hours of both the tides in a day occur at around six in the morning and six at night, then bait digging is, to say the least, very difficult. I have dug bait by the light of a paraffin pressure lamp, but I do not recommend it. It is also a rather dodgy business to be wandering around on a remote shoreline in the dark with the tide coming in and perhaps a few deep gullies between where you are digging and high firm ground.

Early in his shorecasting career, the cost-conscious sea angler will be faced with the 'dig or buy' dilemma. By digging or collecting your bait you will save lots of cash and always be assured of a good supply, regardless of the vagaries of the commercial bait market, but there are naturally some drawbacks. Time is the most important factor. Frequently you will be down on the tideline looking for bait when the fish are biting madly and all your friends who have bought their bait are taking a bag-full of fish. Then the following day when you wake up all eager to get down to the beach with your lovely supply of great big lugworms, you find that an overnight gale has sprung up and mountainous seas are making fishing impossible.

Not all areas with good fish-producing potential have also good bait-digging grounds in the immediate vicinity and anglers often have to travel quite long distances by car to dig their bait. This is where economics become important. Is it cheaper to buy the bait than motor perhaps fifty or sixty miles each way to dig or collect your own?

After many years down on the tideline with fork in hand and back well bent, my final sentiments on the subject are as follows. If you can afford to buy your bait and it is of a high quality, from a reliable source, then do so; it saves a lot of hard, time-consuming work. But if your cash is in short supply and you have plenty of time on your hands, get down there on the littoral and discover what bait digging or collecting is all about. In the process you will learn a great deal about life on the tideline. Your continued observations of the tides, the winds, the waves and the weather will inestimably aid your fish-catching ability. Last, but very important, once your hands become hard and your back used to the unaccustomed toil, you will thoroughly enjoy the whole business.

To end this chapter on the buying of tackle, before I begin to deal specifically with the most suitable rods and reels for all the different types of shore angling, I feel it my duty to give a general résumé of all the separate items of shorefishing tackle which may be needed by an angler who is just taking up the sport. It is most important in these times of continually rising prices to pass on a few timely recommendations on how to purchase all you need at the lowest possible prices, while still maintaining a high standard of quality in everything that is bought.

Since rods and reels are the most expensive items, I will deal with them first. So far as reels are concerned, I regret to say that they have not yet entered the 'assemble it yourself' field. No great price reduction can therefore be obtained in this respect. However, there are other avenues open to the circumspect buyer. A quick glance through the advertising pages of the weekly and monthly angling magazines mentioned earlier will reveal that a never-ending price war goes on in the retail fishing tackle world, with everyone trying to undercut his rival to the benefit of the angler purchaser.

Generally, by comparing the prices of all the 'bargain offer' advertisers, and choosing the best, the astute angler can save himself up to one third of the recommended retail price, which can easily be checked for authenticity by referring to an up-to-date fishing tackle catalogue. As a humorous aside which I find most enlightening, some of these 'cut price tackle merchants' promise to beat any other competitive offer, if the buyer can provide written proof of it.

When considering shorecasting rods, the buyer will immediately discover that just a few of the prices are really astronomical—so high in fact as to suggest a printer's error. For instance, I have before me a list of beachcasting rods, one of which is five times as high in price as all the rest. By looking hard at the description of it, the magical word CARBON or the abbreviated C/F or even C will be noted. Unless you are a millionaire, have just robbed a bank, or been left a substantial legacy by a rich relative, I am sure you will not be interested in paying such a price, which in cold, hard cash represents the price of a whole, comprehensive shorecasting outfit, apart from a brand new, ready-made-up rod. There are two other avenues to explore in the purchasing of a rod—the kit DIY outfit which always gives a very considerable saving and the second-hand market, on which I will expound in the next paragraph or two.

Like certain car owners, people with boats, hi-fi addicts and even dog fanciers who continually strive to be in fashion, the angling world has its share of fishermen who just cannot face up to life without 'This Year's Latest Model', whether it be rod, reel, waterproof jacket or even an 'As Seen on TV' pair of waders. The end-product of all this chopping and changing is evidenced in a very healthy second-hand tackle market. Some tackle dealers even organise separate 'part used' sections on their premises, and I must admit to browsing around for hours in some of them, from which I invariably emerge with a marvellous bargain.

At the present time, *Angler's Mail* are also running, for the benefit of private advertisers, a 'For Sale, Swap or Wanted' page, the contents of which are so interesting that I usually read them before anything else. In these columns can be found a great many very useful, rare, ancient or obsolete items of fishing tackle. Some poor soul with a favourite reel now out of production can often locate and obtain spare parts for it by placing an SOS advert in this excellent angler's 'swap shop' page.

3
Rod Types and How to Choose Them

Fishing tackle catalogues and the proprietors of angling shops usually group rods into three different categories – coarse, sea and game – but they are all basically similar in construction and design and lots of them can be considered interchangeable so far as use is concerned. To give a simple example of what I mean: for pike fishing I often use a beachcasting rod which is designed to throw a 6oz lead in excess of 100 yards, the reason being that, on some specific occasions, I like to use a large herring deadbait which weighs around the ½lb mark and cast it to a distance of about 70 yards on a very deep gravel pit. Conversely, when bass fishing among rocks, weed beds and small patches of open sand and shingle, on a beach where there is no powerful run of the tide, I take with me one of a pair of identical carp rods. It is 11ft long and designed to be matched up to lines of between 8 and 15lb breaking strain and capable of handling a casting weight of about 2½oz.

At the other end of the scale, my favourite coarse fishing rod, a 14½ft hollow glass model which will handle large chub, tench and bream, is often called into use when I am fishing in tidal estuaries, rivers and harbours for mullet, school bass, plaice and dabs. Similarly, a powerful salmon spinning rod will throw a 1½oz self-weighted wobbling lure to a bass from a rocky headland with just the same accuracy and efficiency as it would to a salmon on a big fast-flowing river, and play and land either fish just as well. Therefore, when considering suitable rods for the many different facets of shorefishing, it is wise to evaluate first and foremost how they actually perform and forget what they were originally intended for.

Rod selection is a very personal thing. A well chosen rod intended for casting long distances should feel really comfortable and psychologically 'just right'. If all the time it is in use the angler is battling with a constant, uneasy impression in his mind that he is having to adjust his physical actions to suit the performance of the rod and its dictates, then an unwise choice has been made and a change is necessary. For this precise reason, a great many tackle dealers are now arranging for a 'try out' field, quite near their premises, to be made available. Such a sensible facility builds up a very good, sound customer-salesman relationship and does a great deal towards smoothing the path of the first-time fishing rod buyer, who is prepared to spend a little time and effort in purchasing exactly what is suitable for him.

A whole glossary of angling jargon has been coined by fishermen and rodmakers in an attempt to describe fully and accurately the performance, casting weight range and suitable line strength of the rods now available, especially those designed to propel casting weights in the 3 to 6oz range for long distances. The specifications given for rods in angling catalogues and advertisements are usually so abbreviated as to render them unintelligible to the average layman. A great deal of misconception is often caused in the minds of tackle purchasers by this infuriating business of 'trade terminology'. In order to clarify the situation and ensure that readers of this book, at least, have a working knowledge of 'test curves', 'compound tapers', 'soft-action', 'through action', 'wall thickness' and 'tip velocity', to name but a few rodmaker's terms, I will attempt to put in a nutshell the method used in manufacturing both hollow glass and carbon fibre rod 'blanks'. Once this process is fully understood the mystique of rod jargon will no longer be troublesome.

The very first fibre glass rods were solid and rather heavy, and they were manufactured by a drawing process. From this early pioneering method evolved the modern process of using woven fibre glass cloth impregnated with resin, which is meticulously wrapped round a steel mandrel and bound very tightly so that it follows the shape of the mandrel absolutely accurately. It is then placed in an oven at a high temperature for 'curing'. After this process, the mandrel, or former (which itself closely resembles a very heavy steel fishing rod), is withdrawn from inside the hollow glass rod blank, which is then ground and finished to a perfectly smooth, flawless piece of workmanship.

What is termed the 'action' of the rod (how it flexes and recovers during casting, or responds to the weight of a fish on the line) can be built into the rod blank in the manufacturing and finishing process by a number of different methods. One is by varying the taper of the mandrel around which the fibre glass cloth is wrapped, and another by giving the rod blank thick or thin 'walls'. The very first hollow glass surfcasting rods were made with what is known as a 'slow straight taper' and also a 'slow straight reverse taper'. Slow straight taper rod blanks tapered slowly from butt to tip and the wall thickness was identical throughout their length. Slow straight reverse taper rods were manufactured on more or less the same principle, but the difference in their design was that the top part of the rod tapered from the reel position to the tip and an additional taper was made from the reel fitting down to the butt of the rod. This type of rod blank had a 'bow' casting action; not only did the top part, above the reel, flex, the butt section did also. These rods, of which there are still a few to be had, especially on the second-hand market, are what is termed very 'forgiving' to the amateur shorecaster. Their action is very 'slow', in view of the fact that the whole rod comes under compression during casting. More important still, their 'recovery' is likewise very slow. This type of action in a rod will iron out some of the jerkiness in the faulty casting of a raw beginner and give him some leeway so that he does not 'crack-off' his lead and suffer a line breakage every time he makes a badly mistimed cast.

As the rod blank making industry in this country improved its methods, the advance in technology allowed a far greater latitude for experimentation and rod designs became far more complex.

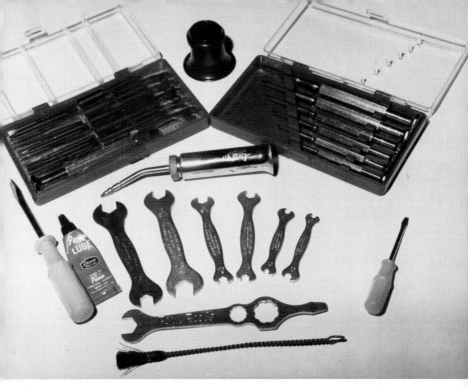

The right tools in the correct sizes for reel servicing. Expensive beach-casting reels do not take kindly to being butchered with pliers, oversize screwdrivers and shifting spanners

By purchasing two sets of rod blanks a perfect 'matched' pair of rods can be made by the DIY angler

Good illumination, the correct tools and a white surface to work over, plus a jeweller's eye-glass, are essentials for efficient reel servicing

Lead casting can be dangerous. Always wear industrial spectacles and, for quick moulding operations, fit the mould with large wooden handles. Never dunk the mould into water to cool it off – moisture and molten lead are a fatal combination

Whereas the old-type rods had slow straight tapers and uniformly thick walls, the more recent types have gradually gone over to medium, fast, and ultra-fast tapers, with the wall thickness having quite a number of variations according to the precise design of the rod blank and the casting action it is intended to have.

To remove some of the mystique from the modern world of rod blank types, I will list the most commonly known kinds and then give a brief résumé of the kind of fishing rods they make. First, we have our old friends the slow straight taper blanks, which have an even wall thickness throughout. A variation on that design is the slow compound taper blank where the wall thickness varies from tip to butt—thick at the bottom and thin at the rod tip. In the fast taper blank category we have the same wall thickness variation. One blank—the fast straight taper—has even wall thickness from butt to tip; the other—the fast compound taper—has a variation, with thick walls at the bottom and thin at the top. There is yet another fast compound taper blank design, where the walls can vary in thickness in different sections of the blank and there can also be a variation in taper in certain sections.

To move on from the design of rod blanks to 'test curves' is a natural progression because the two are very much interrelated. Many years ago, when all rods were made of either solid timber sections or split or whole cane, their 'power' was almost impossible to estimate from their appearance. What happened then was sometimes most embarrassing. A rod could be used in conjunction with a line which was considered (mostly by educated conjecture) suitable in breaking strain, and some surprising things often took place. If the line was far too strong for the rod, then it was inevitable that when great pressure was exerted by the angler, either in casting, playing a fish or pulling out from a snag, the rod broke (sometimes landing the unfortunate fisherman flat on his back among the rocks with his heels in the air). Conversely, when an overpowered rod was used with a line which was too weak for it, the line broke easily on the cast when a fish was struck or being played, or when the terminal tackle got stuck on the bottom. Either way it was a distressing business, and not conducive to good carefree fishing.

Just after World War II, an amazing transformation in the tackle industry took place, sparked off by a few forward-thinking anglers (mostly in the coarse fishing specimen hunting camp) who began to revolutionise rod design. The accent was placed on properly 'balanced' tackle. With the advent of nylon monofilament line in reliably predictable breaking strains, the term 'test curve' emerged. In theory this is the pull, in pounds, required to bend the top section of an upright rod round to an angle of 90 degrees. The popular, simple method of arriving at this measurement on a rod is to attach a strong piece of fishing line or cord to the tip ring and then tie a reliable spring balance to the other end; place the rod firmly, with someone holding it, against a perpendicular wall, goal post or some other structure which is quite plumb, and then have the rod-testing person pull on the spring balance until the top section of the rod comes down parallel with the ground. When this 90 degree angle is formed with the upright butt section of the rod, the poundage reading of the rod is taken. This is an important figure. First and foremost it gives the 'test curve' of the rod, which, if multiplied by five, gives the approximate strength in pounds of the most suitable line strength for it. The 'test curve' figure is also a very accurate guide to the optimum weight in ounces which the rod will cast – one ounce per pound of 'test curve' being the correct figure to apply.

It must be borne in mind that the figure 5, as a multiplication factor for applying to the 'test curve' of a rod to give a recommended line strength, is merely an approximate one. To enlarge on the 'test curve' method further and produce a maximum and minimum line strength range, the test curve poundage can be multiplied by 6 and then 4. As an example, for a beachcaster rod with a 6lb test curve which would comfortably cast a 6oz weight, the minimum line strength would be 24lb ($4 \times 6 = 24$) and the maximum 36lb ($6 \times 6 = 36$).

Now that the rod-making theory has been adequately

expounded and most of the tackle trade technological jargon explained, we can proceed to investigate the different kinds of rods used by the shorefishing sea angler and consider what points to bear in mind when buying them either new, second-hand, or in kit form to be made up by a DIY project.

In view of the fact that roughly half the shorecasting situations around our coastline call for heavy leads to combat the strong tidal flow and also to put the bait well out among the feeding fish, I will deal first with what are known as beachcasting or surfcasting rods. The ready made-up rods, and also the DIY blank sets, are usually in a length range of between 11 and 13ft, and they are described with their casting weight range, for example 11ft bass rod 2–4oz suitable for lines 12–18lb, 12½ft surfcaster 3–5oz suitable for lines 12–25lb, 13ft heavy surfcaster 6–9oz suitable for lines 20–35lb, etc. They are also often described by a much abbreviated selection of codes which are sometimes very baffling. For instance, the tapers of the blanks will be given as S/T for slow taper, M/T for medium taper, F/T for fast taper, and U/F/T for ultra-fast taper. T/W means thin walled, S/U 'stepped up' (more powerful), C/T Carbon fibre tip, with the word 'Fuji's' meaning that the rod has the latest Fuji rings.

Some of the rods advertised will be recommended for casting with fixed-spool reels. These are easily distinguishable from those suitable for use with multiplier reels, as they have only a few very large diameter rings on them and the reel seat position is invariably much lower down the rod than those for multipliers. One point which is baffling to the average newcomer to sea angling is the casting weight ranges given for the rods, which are sometimes put on the rod near the butt in the form of a transfer. Although some rods merely state a very close ratio casting weight, say 1–3oz, 4–6oz or 7–9oz, the figures on some rods will be quite wide, perhaps 2–9oz. Such figures are intended as a rough guide only. With a 2oz weight the rod would be grossly underloaded and would not perform very well. At the other end of the scale, with a 9oz weight it would be vastly overloaded and cast in a very strained, sluggish manner. Most probably the optimum casting weight for a rod described as 2–9oz would be either a 5 or 6oz weight.

One good reason for making up a DIY surfcasting rod, as opposed to buying one 'off the peg' or from the rod rack, is to have it 'tailored' to your exact requirements so far as the fittings, length, weight, and 'action' are concerned. Short squat anglers with short arms will not feel comfortable with a 13ft beachcaster, with the reel position permanently fixed at a distance of 40in up the rod. Generally, anglers under the height of 5ft 8in perform much better with a rod around the 11ft mark, whereas the beefy 6ft-plus fisherman can usually handle rods right up to the 14ft mark without feeling at all ill at ease.

Fast and ultra-fast, steep-tapered, thin-walled surfcasting rods are very exacting in their casting action. By the very nature of their construction their top section does most of the casting work and this makes their 'tip velocity' very fast indeed. By the term 'tip velocity' I mean the speed at which the rod tip section recovers and moves forward after it has been fully compressed by the lead weight into its casting arc. To complicate further the question of the beginner choosing his first beachcasting rod, some ultra-fast rods have been made with rigid butts to give absolute stiffness at the lower end of the rod. This butt rigidity is achieved by fusing into the lower section of the rod blank (part of which is shortened) a 4ft length of dural, or high tensile strength, 14 gauge aluminium. To the highly competent 'tournament style' caster these rods are a dream of pure delight. However, in the hands of a raw beginner the dream of pure delight can be nothing more than an horrific nightmare if he unsuspectingly buys such a rod and attempts to learn to cast with it.

To round off this knotty problem of which beachcaster to buy, I will offer a few broad guidelines for the first-time rod buyer. First and foremost, proceed with great caution. Before parting with your cash, handle all the rods you possibly can and talk to as many knowledgeable beachcasting experts as possible. Plump every time for a slow or medium action rod with reasonably thick walls. Fast taper rods are for competent casters and thin walled blanks fracture easily if not handled with great care. And that does not just mean whilst fishing. I have seen a brand new, high priced thin walled rod badly damaged by a thoughtless angler who tensioned the fastenings on his car roof rack too tightly when fixing the rod into position for a journey to the coast.

On the subject of carbon fibre I am very wary. Carbon and carbon/glass amalgamations are still in their infancy and the present high prices must fall drastically if this type of rod is going to find a ready market. I have tried a few glass rods with carbon tips, however, and find them a joy to use – good for casting performance and very sensitive in their extra thin tip section.

One very sobering aspect of the rod blank industry is the fact that, as the output of the separate manufacturers runs into many thousands for each particular type, identical blanks are bought by different rod finishing firms and put out under various names – sometimes with widely dissimilar performance specifications. A rod may appear glowingly termed 'Joe Blogg's Beachmaster Special: 4–6oz', while an identical blank from the same manufacturing source but finished by another of their trade outlets may rejoice in the name 'Harry Higgins' 200yd Super Surf Shooter: 2–9oz' – all very bewildering to the angler with no precise idea of the kind of rod which will suit him best.

I am delighted to note these days, when I spend an hour or two browsing through rod racks in tackle shops, that those angling monstrosities known in years gone by as 'pier rods' have largely disappeared from the shorecasting scene. They were very stout (about 9ft long) and completely unbending unless a huge conger eel in the 50 or 60lb weight range was hooked. Only then did they give a little. I do not mourn the passing of such unsuitable items. A serviceable and very cheap pier or harbour wall fishing rod can be adapted from a good long-butted, slow taper beachcaster, and there are plenty of excellent ones on the second-hand market these days. Where long casting is not required, but heavy terminal tackle is, such a rod, with a foot or so cut off from the butt end to make it more manageable for propping upright against the pier rails, will make an ideal tool for the job.

Any angler with a comprehensive set of coarse fishing tackle will be delighted to find that the whole of it can be adapted to the shore angling scene with great success. Modern carp and pike 'specimen hunting' rods which are usually around the 11ft mark, with a test curve of about 2lb and designed to handle lines in the 8–12lb breaking strain category and cast 2 or 3oz, are absolutely ideal for bass fishing where there is no strong run of tide on a shoreline where a 2 or 3oz Arlesey bomb will hold bottom comfortably.

Likewise, these rods, when used in conjunction with the normal coarse fish, specimen hunting, fixed-spool reels with interchangeable spools of line in the 8, 10 and 12lb breaking strain range, will make an ideal tackle combination for spinning from piers, harbour walls, jetties, groynes and rocky headlands which give onto deep water. Such an outfit is also quite suitable for what I shall term medium saltwater float fishing. The locations I have in mind are those where large flat tables of rock enable the angler to fish into deep water very close to his angling stance, and long casting is not called for. I have fished such venues for wrasse around the Cornish coastline and used the identical tackle which has served me well on coarse fishing waters for pike livebaiting, the only alteration being the bait, which was either a hardback crab or a live prawn hooked once through the tail. Incidentally, where the fishing position is quite close to the water level and the rocks are not too dangerous, I have found that a long-handled coarse fishing landing net will do an admirable job of getting the hooked fish out of the water safely. This avoids putting too much strain on the rod tip by trying to lift the fish direct from the water with the rod bent in an alarmingly tight curve.

The rods used in conjunction with Scarborough reels are not generally available in tackle shops all round the coastline. Like certain other items of tackle, which have a strong tradition of local usage, they are to be found only in shops at their places of origin. The 'blanks' for Scarborough type sea rods can sometimes be obtained on the Yorkshire coast at tackle shops in Whitby, Scarborough and Bridlington. But as they are of such a special design, the majority of rod blank manufacturers overlook them.

Basically, the rod which is matched to the famous 'cart wheel' Scarborough reel (which I shall deal with in more detail in the next chapter) is a very stiff, powerful 'pulley-hauling' pole in thick walled hollow glass between 9 and 11ft in length. Power – rather than casting and fish playing ability – is the secret of its performance. It is designed primarily for exceedingly rough, snaggy shorelines rather than fishing finesse.

Finally, to round off this collection of rods suitable for shorefishing, I must mention a whole host of situations which call for a very light tackle approach and for which the lightest of coarse fishing rods fits the bill admirably. For instance, where it is necessary to angle from harbour walls, or in estuaries, perhaps with float tackle, or very light leads on the bottom when there is no great strength of tide run and the species being sought are not very large, then the modern match, swing-tip, leger and spinning rods are the ideal tools to use. They should be coupled of course with their appropriate freshwater reels, and used with coarse-fishing floats, hooks, lines and split shot or leger weights.

One very successful method of taking sea fish from the shoreline is by adapting fly-fishing tactics and tackle to the sea fishing scene. Mackerel, garfish, mullet, pollack, coalfish and bass will all, at the appropriate times of clear water and calm, summer weather, take both floating and sub-surface fished flies and lures.

A necessary warning, however, to those readers who have not previously used their treasured coarse or fly-fishing gear in the sea: saltwater corrosion is deadly if it is allowed to attack your tackle. All items used for sea angling should be well washed in fresh water and carefully dried and oiled before being stored away. Particular attention must be paid to rod bags or reel cases which are either wet or impregnated with saltwater spray. It is no use carefully cleaning your rod and reel and giving them a thorough drying off if they are then put into a wet bag or case.

4
Suitable Reels for Shorefishing

Although the rods for shorefishing are many and varied in price, design, construction, length and finish, they are all built on basically the same lines, with rod blanks, rings, reel fittings and some kind of handle grip or butt covering. Reels, however, are quite different. There are four models currently in use for shorefishing: the fixed-spool, multiplier, side-cast and centre-pin, and each one is very different in construction, appearance and method of operation. The two most popular, the multiplier and the fixed-spool, are completely dissimilar in both mechanical form and appearance, not to mention price – the multiplier usually costs about twice as much as the fixed-spool reel.

Up to a few years ago, the users of multiplier reels considered themselves the absolute elite of the beachcasting fraternity. Such were their feelings of superiority that they were apt to refer to the fixed-spool devotees as 'coffee-grinders' and 'egg-beaters'. Happily, however, the much maligned fixed-spool reels have recently become so improved in design and performance that even the multiplier fanatics of yesteryear are now to be found down on the tideline using them when the conditions for which they are best suited prevail.

The multiplier reel, by virtue of its direct line feed onto a revolving spool when reeling in, and its 'in line' release of line, through the rod rings, when casting is being done, is considered more efficient in those respects than the fixed-spool reel. The very latest, high precision multipliers also feature an automatic gear shift which gives a normal retrieve of about 4 to 1, which drops down automatically to a slower retrieve of 2½ to 1 if a heavy fish is hooked and is fighting strongly. Conversely, should the fish change direction suddenly, and run in fast towards the angler, thereby reducing the tension of the line, the reel then 'thinks' for itself and ups the gear ratio to 4 to 1 again to enable the angler to keep in contact with his quarry.

The one great drawback to multiplier reels, especially in the untutored hands of amateur shorecasters, is a dreaded malady called the over-run. Put briefly, it is a shocking tangle of line all round the reel spool which is commonly referred to as a 'bird's nest'. This is a direct result of the reel continuing to throw off line faster than the flying lead can take it. It usually occurs towards the end of the casting sequence, but it can also occur right at the beginning, and indeed at any time during the cast, if the casting style is jerky rather than smooth, controlled and perfectly co-ordinated. During casting with a multiplier reel, the speed of the revolving drum which is releasing the line is invariably controlled by the angler's thumb. Surfcasting experts, who are now casting up to and over the 200yd mark, are known to have what are called in angling parlance 'educated thumbs'; lots of casting practice has given them the ability to control the multiplier reel spool with amazing finesse.

To overcome this inherent, and decidedly off-putting, tendency of the multiplier reel to create disastrous line-tangling over-runs, the manufacturers of the high precision (and extremely expensive) models have built into their reels various braking mechanisms, in an attempt to compensate for faulty casting. Centrifugal brakes with different sizes of brake blocks for strong, medium and light correction are incorporated into modern multiplier reel designs to take care of the running of the spool at high revolutions. For low revolution running of the spool, a mechanical adjustable brake is also fitted, with 'click stops' to balance the running of the spool to different casting weights. A further refinement on some multiplier reels is a 'level-wind' system, which mechanically moves the line evenly to and fro across the whole width of the spool. To enable the multiplier reel to operate with a safety margin line release, in order to avoid

45

a sudden line breakage if a strong, heavy fish is making a rapid run seawards or if one is being played in heavy surf, a 'star-drag' spool release mechanism is also fitted. This works on a compression chain system of cork or leather washers and thin metal plates. By tightening up the 'star-drag' adjuster to just below the breaking strain of the line on the spool, a heavy fish can be wound in or played on the reel handle, but there is always a 'slipping clutch' safety mechanism in operation ready to release line should a break be imminent.

It is absolutely vital, when considering the purchase of a multiplier reel to be used for long casting from the shoreline, to ensure that two important points are firmly understood. The reel must be a shorecasting or surfcasting model with a lightweight spool – not a boat fishing model with a heavy metal spool. Also, it is essential that the reel has what is termed 'one screw take-apart', which means that the spools can be changed very rapidly and easily without tools having to be used or lots of fiddly screws removed.

Now let us appraise that popular 'maid of all work' and friend of inexperienced beachcasters: the fixed-spool reel. It will bring instant long-casting ability to the most hamfisted shoreline operator – hence its great popularity. The secret of its trouble-free line release lies in the fact that it does not have a spool which revolves during the cast – hence its name the fixed-spool reel. Unlike the multiplier, which has its spool revolving and feeding line direct through the rod rings, the spool of the fixed-spool reel is mounted pointing directly up the rod towards the rings. During the cast, the revolving bale arm (which pushes line onto the spool during the retrieve) is folded back so that the line can spill over the end of the spool at exactly the speed of the sinker which is pulling it off. By this means the problem of spool inertia is completely eliminated. A badly timed, snatchy cast merely sends the terminal tackle forward with a jerk which whips off coils of line over the end of the spool. Unlike the multiplier, the spool of which would instantly revolve at a great rate and throw off a great deal of tangle-making line, the fixed-spool reel, with its

46

non-revolving spool and trouble-free line release, copes with the angler's errors quite competently.

Having enumerated all the advantages of the fixed-spool reel for shorecasting, I will now list its drawbacks so that the inexperienced angler will not be deluded into thinking such reels are the complete answer to all casting problems. Without a doubt, I think that the most off-putting aspect of the fixed-spool reel is its unnervingly noisy line release and the failure of the bale arm sometimes to stay folded back during the action of casting. This last fault has been completely eliminated on some models with an anti-inertia lock system which is absolutely effective in operation. However, some reels still have the infuriating habit of the bale arm snapping forward right at the beginning of the cast when the line is flying off at great speed and the lead is zooming skywards. Such a catastrophic event completely undermines your confidence, of course. Just when you think you are about to break all casting records, your line breaks instead, with a sharp crack like a pistol shot, and the terminal tackle wings its way towards the far horizon, right out among the feeding fish. Unfortunately you and the 'bottom end' of your gear are now completely unattached.

Fixed-spool reels and heavy line are quite incompatible, however. For shorecasting situations where line in the breaking strains of between 18 and 22lb (0.45mm to 0.50mm line thickness) can safely be used, fixed-spool reels have definite casting advantages over the multiplier so far as the beginner is concerned. But the spool of the fixed-spool reel must be loaded with line correctly and this factor is of vital importance if good, trouble-free, long casts are to be made. To reach the peak of casting performance the line must be loaded on to the spool until there is no more than ⅛in of spool lip standing proud above it at the front 'spill-off' edge. A half-filled spool reduces casting distance enormously, because the line has to jump out of the deep spool-well as each yard peels off and this constant friction of the line over the spool lip slows down the terminal tackle.

Just as the multiplier reel has a 'safety factor' against line breakage with its 'star-drag' spool release mechanism, so the fixed-spool reel has what is called a 'slipping clutch'. If this is adjusted correctly, the spool, which does not normally revolve, will turn and release line as the breaking strain is reached, which gives the angler a built-in safety margin against losing a big fish. Unfortunately this 'slipping-clutch' mechanism can prove disastrous when a cast is being made if the angler does not remember to tighten up the slipping clutch before making his cast so that the spool is locked absolutely tight and is unable to move no matter how much power is put into the cast.

What happens if the spool is not positively locked tight is one of the most confidence-destroying aspects of fixed-spool casting. The angler takes up his casting stance and adjusts the length of terminal tackle 'drop' from rod tip to sinker. He then opens the reel bale arm and folds it back into the casting position, at the same time trapping the line near the spool in the crook of the first joint of his index finger. Then he prepares to cast and unfortunately, just as he has reached maximum compression with the rod in a beautiful arc, the power of the cast proves too much for the slack slipping clutch and it releases perhaps a short length of line which is under great tension. Naturally this line slices deeply into the flesh of that very vulnerable forefinger, and sometimes the angler has his confidence in fixed-spool reels shattered for ever more. To prevent such distressing accidents, there are quite a number of precautionary measures which can be taken. A leather finger-stall over the index finger is a good protection. So also is a wrapping of surgical tape. The ultimate safety device, however, is a small invention called a 'thumb button' which, when whipped to the rod quite near to the reel spool, provides an absolutely safe and foolproof mechanical line release. I shall refer again to this valuable casting attachment in the chapter dealing with safe, trouble-free casting.

One problem with fixed-spool reels, so far as casting performance is concerned, is the correct ringing of the rod with which they are to be used. There are two separate schools of thought on this subject, and, to be quite honest, I have after a great deal of experimentation been unable, to date, to come up with the correct answer myself. The 'large diameter ring' school of thought propounds that the rod should have no more than five rings on it, which should be very large in diameter, with the butt ring quite near to the reel in order to smooth out the flying coils and get the line under control as it flows up the rod through the rest of the rings. Unfortunately, these large diameter rings fail to prevent what is called 'line slap' – the off-putting noise made by the line as it flies off the reel spool in loose coils and hits the rod on its way up through the rings. The suggested answer to this noisy and friction-producing line release drawback is to reduce the diameter of the five rings and place the first one some distance away from the reel spool, offset from the rod, so that it is as near in line with the centre of the reel spool as possible. The theory behind this method appears sound enough. The smaller offset ring opposite the reel spool cones the spirals of line which fly off the reel during the cast and straightens them out so that they run in a controlled manner up the rod rings.

After extensive casting experiments with fixed-spool reels on rods ringed in both styles, I would offer the following observations but no absolute conclusion on which is the better method. First, the rod with the large rings, although producing lots of casting noise, does seem to retard the line less than the other one. Second, the rod with the smaller rings, whilst effectively 'coning' the line and reducing the noisy 'line slap', does seem to have a great deal of friction generated at the first ring, which certainly straightens out the flying spirals of line but I would think cuts down the distance of the cast.

Having thoroughly investigated the two most popular shore-casting reels in use today, it is now time to give some thought to a couple of 'minority group' reels, the first of which is the side-cast. My own assessment of this reel, which originates in Australia where it is very popular for heavy surfcasting, is that it is an ingenious compromise between the fixed-spool reel and a single action centre-pin. To gain full advantage of the side-cast reel it is usually mounted fairly low on the rod butt. Here I find it

49

necessary to issue a solemn warning about the security of the reel fitting to house it. As the surfcasting side-cast reel is a somewhat heavy cumbersome piece of angling equipment, the reel fitting needs to be of the positive screw-locking type. The modern Fuji snaplock fittings may be quite adequate to retain multiplier and fixed-spool reels during vigorous casting, but after seeing a brand new side-cast reel leap out of such a reel fitting, bounce with a sickening crash onto a concrete jetty and then take a dive into the sea, from where its unfortunate owner retrieved it in a sorry damaged state, I feel it my duty to make a strong point about the security of the fitting.

In appearance the side-cast reel is just like a large wide-drummed boat reel, and is mounted in traditional fashion on the rod like a big centre-pin reel. When line is retrieved it operates with the same direct 'onto the spool' winching method. But when a cast is being made, by a well designed swivel mounting incorporated into the rod fitting bracket, the reel can be turned sideways on to the rod, to put it into the position of the fixed-spool reel so that the line flies off over the end of the spool in exactly the same release method as the fixed-spool reel.

After the cast, the reel is swung back into its original 'fore-and-aft' position and the line is then reeled back just like the operation of a centre-pin reel. Like the fixed-spool reel, the side-cast is a boon to any angler who fears using a multiplier because of its shocking tendency to backlash or over-run when a cast is being made. One great advantage of the side-cast to a shore angler who is after large fish which run far and fast – tope for instance – is its enormous line capacity. The popular model for heavy shore fishing has a 6in diameter spool which is 2½in wide, and it will comfortably take 600 yards of 15lb line, 400 yards of 20lb, or 300 yards of 30lb.

The last reel in this group of four which are all designed for shorefishing with heavy tackle is the 'Scarborough'. As I have said, it is so specialised and local in its use that it will seldom be found in tackle catalogues or in the windows of tackle shops outside the area in which it is most used. Basically, the

Scarborough reel is the most simple, unmechanical piece of angling equipment ever designed (perhaps that word 'designed' should be 'evolved'). It is nothing more than a large wooden wheel with a deep line groove round the outer circumference, two winding handles, a centre spindle, and a rod mounting bracket. Some of the latest models have a twin ball-race centre mounting, in place of the old, traditional brass bush and spindle, and they are made up from 'tuffnol' instead of being turned in one piece from a block of hard walnut. However they are constructed, there is very little on them to go wrong or cause the angler the slightest trouble, even though they are often subjected to the gravest of misuse. The only maintenance they should ever need is an occasional squirt of oil onto the running mechanism, be it brass bush and steel spindle or double ball-race with spindle housing. With no gears to damage, an angler using a Scarborough reel set-up can lie back on his rod, if the tackle becomes snagged or a fish dives into dense kelp, and heave to his heart's content. He is safe in the knowledge that, as long as the line holds, he can exert as much pressure as he likes without 'stripping' the innards of his reel, which is what would happen if it was a multiplier with the anti-reverse engaged.

For the lighter styles of shorefishing, where heavy surfcasting with weighty leads is not required, a whole range of reels can be used: small multipliers and medium-sized fixed-spool reels for spinning, float fishing and light lead casting; also freshwater fishing centre-pin reels which are especially efficient when a down-tide float trotting technique is being employed. I find that a 5in 'Leeds' centre-pin reel (which is another Yorkshire speciality) is particularly effective for rivermouth and harbour mullet fishing, where coarse fishing methods and tackle are the only way by which these enigmatic fish can be taken successfully.

At the risk of labouring a theme, I must stress that saltwater and high precision mechanical parts made of metal do not mix happily. It may not be harmful for a coarse or fly fisherman to dump his wet tackle into a dark corner of a cupboard and leave it until required for the next outing. But if you are a sea angler, don't think you can follow such behaviour. In the interim period, the sea angler's tackle could well be badly corroded so far as the moving, mechanical parts are concerned, and deeply pitted by saltwater action on the bright chrome outer casings. A good swilling with warm fresh water, proper drying and re-oiling is the only method I know to combat the saltwater menace.

A few timely hints on the subject of service and replacement parts are, I feel, of vital importance. If you buy your reel at a greatly reduced price from a mail order source of supply, do not expect to be received with open arms by your local tackle dealer if it breaks down. In view of the fact that you have made a considerable saving on the initial purchase, he will expect you to have the decency to send it back to the makers to have it put right, and thereby hangs many a sorry tale. Do not ever, under any circumstances, purchase a reel which cannot be repaired quickly (in days – not weeks or months) in this country. To be safe in your choice, I would recommend you to buy the most popular, widely used reel possible, from a reputable maker. A test of the immediate availability of spares and service can be done quite easily. When considering the reel in the tackle shop, casually ask the tackle dealer if he can fit minor replacement parts 'while-you-wait' on the premises. If he looks embarrassed, aghast or puzzled and puts you off with some vague excuse such as 'I can't give you a direct answer right now', think twice about the reel *and the tackle dealer*.

One great problem with all multiplier and fixed-spool reels is the knotty subject of what happens when the particular model which you have treasured and cossetted becomes obsolete. Some makers of high repute, to their eternal glory, continue to supply spares and service long after they have ceased to manufacture some of their models. However, many more do not honour their customers with such commendable integrity.

These are just a few points to pay careful regard to when reel buying. I am quite aware that we live in an affluent 'throw away' society, but I find the price of good fishing reels far too high to qualify them for that type of description.

An easily made wooden tripod is best for rocky shorelines. Since this mudflat and rock venue will play havoc with standard angling clothing it is best to wear old, washable working garments

A well designed monopod should hold the rod steady, with the handle and reel at the right level for an 'instant grab'. The rod rest should be stable enough to hold a few fish as well, if necessary

Four types of rod rest used by the author. From left to right: wooden tripod; commercial angle-iron beach rod rest; specially made 'rough stuff' monopod in heavy mild steel with a strong footbar for driving into stony shorelines; sand spike in lightweight dural

A lightweight angling headlamp with a powerpack that clips to a belt. This gives instant light when surf wading and is safe to use when scaling rocks, especially if companions are climbing below

5
Other Essential Accessories

Having examined the two major and most expensive items of the shorefisher's tackle – rods and reels – consideration should be given to some other accessories which are needed in order that the shorefishing sea angler may be completely equipped.

In a previous chapter, I have already mentioned buying nylon monofilament line in bulk spools for economy, but I feel a little more enlightenment on the subject of nylon fishing line and how to buy it wisely will not come amiss. Although there are literally hundreds of fanciful trade names printed on labels which are stuck on spooled nylon, it may come as a shock to the newcomer to shorefishing to learn that the whole of it is manufactured by just a few wholesalers. These sell in bulk to a great number of distributors who re-spool the line, apply a brand name label, and then supply it to the retail tackle trade. Unknown to the majority of trusting anglers, lots of line which appears under different brand names, is absolutely identical, and from the same manufacturing source. Therefore we often have the ludicrous situation of an angler strongly recommending his favourite brand of line to his friends and saying that another kind is quite useless, when, in fact, if the truth of the matter were revealed, they are one and the same line.

The only sure way for an angler to come to the correct conclusions about the line he is going to use is by purchasing 100yd (or metre) spools of several different brands and personally testing them under actual fishing conditions. Then, having finally decided on the best one, stick to it rigidly and buy it in bulk spools. From past experience, I can say with sincerity that there is nothing more infuriating than to buy a great Jumbo spool of several thousand yards of line, enough to load up your reel a dozen or so times in fact, and then find, to your extreme dismay, that it is the most horribly stiff, springy, tangle-producing stuff ever made.

The secret of high performance nylon monofilament fishing line is strict quality control in all the manufacturing processes. Cheap substandard line usually has great variations in thickness and a molecular structure which lacks what is called 'memory'. Put in plain language, 'memory' really means that, when stretched or distorted and then released, it immediately regains its former structure and strength without going weak and curly.

Good quality nylon monofilament should be smooth without being very shiny and brittle. If it jumps off the spool in watch spring coils that are stiff and unmanageable, beware; it will do the same once you have loaded up your reel with it and cause endless frustrating tangles on the shoreline. Conversely, your new line should not be so soft and limp that the surface will become easily damaged as you reel in your tackle over the sand and shingle. This is where tests with those small 100yd spools will pay dividends. Instead of relying on some other angler's recommendations as to what line you should use, you will know from personal experience what suits you best for the type of fishing you are doing.

It has been said that the hook is actually the most important item of all, because it is the angler's direct and final link with his quarry—the fish. Having lost many good fish through faulty hooks, I can heartily endorse that sentiment. I am sure it is quite safe to say that more fish regain their freedom through faulty hooks than by all the other unfortunate incidents brought about by unsound tackle and incompetent anglers, added together. Good, tried, trusty, well made, properly tempered hooks are a blessing, but bad hooks are a time-wasting temper-fraying menace. Like nylon line, they require testing before the angler puts them into use on his terminal tackle. It is far better to go through a 100 box of hooks and, after carefully examining them and giving them a few simple tests, end up with 50 and the rest in the dustbin than casually use them straight from the box and discover their failings by losing fish.

To anyone who is foolish enough to believe that hooks are sharp when they come from the makers, I would recommend what I term 'the jeweller's eye glass' test. Purchase one of these inexpensive and easily used magnifiers and look at the hook points through it. The points will closely resemble one of the tines on an old, blunt kitchen fork and the hook barb will often appear so 'rank' and badly formed that the angler will be convinced that it would take a sledgehammer to drive it into the jaw of a fish.

The first hook test must be for correct temper. Put the hook 'bend' into a vice with the shank and point protruding and twang it. If it bends and stays bent it is soft; if it breaks it is too brittle. The ones which survive this weeding out process are fit for fish catching, but they still need some work to be done on them. Next, make sure the eye is well formed and properly closed or, with 'spade end' hooks, that the spade is not too big and is not sharp, so that it would cut the line when the hook is knotted to it. Then comes the final sharpening. Hone the hook point to needle sharpness with a small, fine file or a slip of oil or carborundum stone. Then attend to the barb. Reduce its size if it appears to be too large in proportion to the hook, also if it is very deeply cut, so that it goes down right into the metal of the hook. But watch out! Test it at that point in a vice by securing the hook point and giving the shank a sharp twist. If the barb has been too deeply cut, the hook will snap at that place. Hooks for sea angling begin at 1/0 and increase in size as the number also increases. Conversely, hooks in the sizes suitable for coarse fishing (which are much smaller) begin at size 2 and decrease in size as the number increases.

Since the bait used, the fishing conditions, and the species of fish being angled for are the deciding factors which govern hook selection, I shall have a great deal more to say on that aspect of the suitability of various hooks in later chapters.

Highly indispensable items of tackle, especially if you are fishing over what is known as 'tackle-hungry ground', are the lead casting weights used to enable the fisherman to make long casts and have his terminal gear hold bottom in a strong tide. The shape of these weights is of vital importance. After much experimentation, an aerodynamic 'bomb' shape has finally emerged as the most successful. To enable them to take a firm grip in sand, mud and shingle, such sinkers were originally moulded with four grip wires protruding from the nose section. These were ideal for holding the terminal tackle in the tide, but they produced a serious anchor-dragging effect whenever the fisherman began to reel in his tackle. To obviate this serious shortcoming, two very astute and inventive beach anglers produced and patented the 'breakaway' lead. By an ingenious design of loose, pivotting wires and four plastic beads which fitted into corresponding depressions in the nose section of the lead bomb, a successful 'release' was effected when the angler wished to reel in his terminal tackle. Basically the wires that had been protruding at right angles from the lead bomb and anchoring it were sprung from their positions after pressure was applied, and they swivelled in their slots in the lead and trailed astern of it.

A further, very useful addition to the breakaway lead is the recent breakaway sinker adapter. This is a plastic moulding of tough nylon designed to augment the standard breakaway lead so far as tide holding is concerned without adding further casting weight. These sinker adapters look exactly the same as breakaway leads and they work just as efficiently; the only difference is that they are virtually weightless. They are mounted above the lead sinker and have a strong clip in their base so that this can be done effectively. One other good use to which they can be put is to convert plain, unwired sinkers into the 'release anchor' lead category.

Before leaving the subject of lead weights, in the interests of safety a few instructions should be passed on regarding the handling of molten lead. For those thrifty, adventurous, DIY enthusiasts who wish to purchase a sinker-making mould and 'do their own thing', golden rule number one is to wear industrial goggles to protect your eyes. Also, as an extra safety precaution, keep the arms and hands well covered with a thick jersey or jacket, and gauntlet gloves. Hot lead and damp moulds produce disasters – hence the need for goggles. If you are foolish enough to cool your mould to obtain a rapid, production line performance in your sinker casting, watch out for trouble. After you have withdrawn the sinker and clamped the two halves of the mould back together again, there may be tiny drops of water trapped unseen in it. As soon as the pouring of molten lead begins again 'spitting' will occur, and if you have your unprotected face right above the inlet hole and some hot lead comes flying upward, your next move will not be to the beach for a fishing session but to the casualty ward of the nearest hospital. To remain safe and unscarred whilst sinker making, forget all about the water cooling treatment for the mould, by purchasing one which has two countersunk screw holes bored into the clamping faces. These holes enable two 6in broom shaft handles to be screwed to the separate halves of the mould so that the sinkers can be extracted whilst the mould is still hot, without the lead-casting operator getting his hands burned whilst trying to pull the hot mould apart to get the sinker out.

So far as the pouring of the lead is concerned, never take a great pot of molten lead from the heat source and carry it to the mould. Such a practice is highly dangerous should you trip and spill it or accidentally drop it. Get a plumber's ladle and pour your lead in small quantities by dipping the ladle into the main lead melting pot. That way, if you are unfortunate and have a spillage, it will be only with a small quantity of hot lead.

The last hint towards self-preservation is of great importance, and quite a few accidents that I personally know of could have been prevented if this simple observation had been carried out. If you are using old plumbing pipes for sinker making, do not chop them up into short convenient lengths with an axe, so that they will go easily into the melting pot. Should there be any moisture trapped in the pipe, shortly after it is placed into the melting pot the water in the pipe will expand into steam, blow open the ends of the pipe and splatter the whole of the contents of the pot around the room. As an added precaution when using scrap lead pipe for sinker making, cut it open lengthways with shears or a hacksaw and hammer it out flat. Hot molten lead is lethal. Be warned and carry out all lead-casting operations very carefully, concentrating all the time on the job in hand and not letting your attention wander from what you are doing. Molten metal sticks to naked flesh like glue and burns itself into it, leaving very deep and ugly scars.

Sea angling terminal tackle and rigs, especially those for long casting, should have the minimum of accoutrements incorporated into them to enable them to flight freely through the air without causing a lot of wind drag. Wire booms and other unnecessary appendages certainly cut down casting distance, and they also make lost sets of terminal tackle prohibitively expensive when the fishing is being done over snaggy ground. Swivels, however, are a vital necessity, especially when fishing into a strong tidal flow, in order that line tangling may be reduced to a bare minimum. The very best swivels, which are more expensive than the rest but most reliable in their performance, are those which are listed for size and breaking strain as well.

Rust is the recognized arch-enemy of swivels and hooks, and those large multi-drawered cantilever tackle boxes, which every time they are opened expose all the contents, are the worst places for storing such items. This is especially true on an exposed sea shoreline where there is sand and saltwater-laden spray flying around everywhere. Keep your hooks and swivels in small tins or plastic boxes with a liberal amount of pilchard or cod liver oil brushed over them and they will never become tarnished, corroded or rusty. Mineral oils such as motor or household lubricating oils would do the job just as efficiently, but it is my firm belief that their smell is very off-putting to all forms of fish and marine life.

The popular picture postcard portrayal of a shore angler is

usually one where the rod is firmly propped up against a pier safety rail, with the fisherman standing back, smiling, smoking his pipe and eagerly awaiting results. Although such a scene may look very attractive in an angling magazine or on the cover of a tackle catalogue, convenient propping-up places for the angler's rod are few and far between under actual shorefishing conditions. Therefore a secure rod rest is needed, one which will not blow over in a strong gust of wind and let your treasured and expensive beach outfit fall with a sickening crash on to the concrete harbour wall. Or, if fishing on a sandy beach, the rest must hold the rod upright and not let it topple over into the sand, where the reel would definitely suffer from a severe gritting of the works.

Basically, there are just two kinds of rod rests – those in the form of a tripod for harbour walls, promenades and rocky shorelines, and single-leg 'monopods' for soft angling venues where the rod rest, or beach spike, can easily be driven in firmly. There are a great many different kinds of rod-holding appliances available on the tackle market. Those made of metal invariably rust rapidly unless they are heavily proofed with paint or religiously cleaned and greased after every outing. Wooden tripods, made up from hardwood timber with a hinged back leg, are my favourite for places where a monopod cannot be driven into the ground. To give such tripods extra stability in strong winds or to keep them in position when the rod is removed, so that they don't go sailing over the harbour wall into the sea below, I hang half a brick from a stout piece of cord centrally between the three legs so that it just swings clear of the ground.

Monopods need to be very strong and well designed to stand up to the rough treatment they will surely get if they are used on a stony beach. It is vital that they have a stabilising fin or bar situated somewhere near to the point so that when the monopod is driven into the shoreline it is locked firmly into the right position and stays there. Failure to attend to this last detail when buying or designing a monopod will cause serious accidents to your tackle. In a strong tide an ordinary monopod with no stabiliser on it will swing seawards and allow your rod and reel to topple into the surf, or perhaps be dragged seawards by a large fish which suddenly snatches your bait. For the roughest of stony shorelines, I have designed a special heavy duty monopod which is made up from a 3ft length of thick walled, mild steel tubing with the rod-holding cup and bracket welded into position at the top and a 6in length of steel 'footbar' also welded at right angles to the main stem, about 6in from the point at the bottom. This monopod can be driven easily into the hardest of stony shorelines by putting heavy foot pressure onto the locking bar until it is buried right below the sand level.

For fishing from beaches when there is a heavy surf running a tall monopod is necessary, one which elevates the rod tip sufficiently to let the line be lifted as far above the waves as possible. One final precaution which may save you a lost beach fishing outfit. Never stray away from your tackle and leave it to attend to itself. In strong tides, if there are great mats of floating weed about, one of these very heavy weed bunches could become tangled in your line around the terminal rig and the whole lot, rod, reel and monopod be dragged into the sea never to be seen again. Likewise, in the calmest of conditions, a very large fish could become attached to the end of your line and, if you are not close at hand, your rod and reel could suddenly take a lightning dive seawards. The outcome would be decided by how fast you could run in thigh boots into the surf to catch hold of them before they vanished beneath the waves.

Without a doubt, the most productive times for catching fish from the shore are those during the hours of darkness. With the holidaymakers and casual beach wanderers safely tucked up in bed or watching the telly, the shore fisherman has the whole tideline to himself. This topic naturally leads me on to the subject of illumination for the sea angler. As times change and technology becomes more advanced, so do fashions in beach lights. Originally, the old-fashioned hurricane lamp had to suffice, but its light power was poor and those made in cheap, thin tin sheet did not last long amidst sand and salt water. Then came the era of the paraffin pressure storm lantern, and this means of shoreline illumination is still the most popular form of lighting on the beaches today. Although the lamps themselves are not as cheap as they used to be, the fuel price and consumption leave nothing to be desired.

There is one great drawback to the paraffin pressure lamp, and that is its size and weight. For the roving shore angler, it means that one hand is always needed to carry the lamp and if difficult cliff paths or rocks are being negotiated in the dark this could be a problem. An electric headlight would solve the lamp-carrying problem completely. These headlights are also very efficient and extremely helpful when an angler is playing and reeling in a large fish in total darkness. The beam automatically follows the direction of the head; wherever you look you have a good, powerful, illuminating shaft of bright light.

On some parts of the coastline, particularly on headlands, piers, jetties and harbour walls, the use of bright lights by anglers is considered a navigational hazard and they are strictly forbidden. This is where the latest invention of rod tip lights scores. They are tiny tritium-filled luminous tubes which are screwed into a small rod tip adapter whipped to the rod top. The makers claim a life expectancy of about twenty years, by which time I suppose the purchaser will be in a wheel chair and too doddery to go fishing, or something better will have hit the tackle market. These rod tip lights are available in three powers—100, 300 and 500 micro lamberts. I prefer the 300 as I can easily see it at a normal rod watching stance of 15 to 30ft. If you buy one of the 500 strength, you may stray too far from your rod and miss a lot of tip-banging bites.

The angler who wishes to become really proficient at digging his own bait will quickly discover, if he visits quite a number of different bait beds, that each type of geographical location has its own traditional type of digging tool for winkling out the lug or ragworms. Generally the following guidelines hold good: for estuarial mud-flats a broad tined 'spud' fork; for sand the traditional long-handled three-tined lugworm fork; and for deep-boring black lugworms in either sand, mud or a mixture of both, the 'grafter', draining spade or lugworm spade (all the same type of tool).

Some tackle shops, especially where the staff are practising sea anglers, stock all these digging tools. However, at times they cannot be bought and prospective angler bait diggers are nonplussed as to how they can locate a supplier. In such cases, turn your back on the tackle shops and go to any good garden tool supplier and ask to see a manufacturers' catalogue, especially one put out by an old-established firm. I will guarantee that you will be absolutely astounded at the scores of different spades and forks that are available – everything from special peat-digging spades in a variety of designs right through the gardening tools and into bait-digging implements.

Large, sharp knives are very necessary for gutting and filleting the angler's catch. But for the job of cutting lengths of nylon line to make up terminal tackles, especially on windswept beaches by the light of a storm lantern, they can be rather lethal to the fingers, especially if your hands are numb with cold. For all line-snipping jobs, I find a small pair of nail clippers invaluable. They can be kept on a key ring in the pocket of your fishing jacket where they will always be handy. Alternatively, if you are a forgetful person, who is always losing small items, hang them from your jacket zip slide with a split ring. In that position they will be most conveniently situated for cutting line.

On the subject of tackle purchasing, the angler should be wary of 'job-lot' and economy price bulk buying. From time to time in various angling publications, advertising blurbs appear offering fantastic numbers of hooks, or miles of line, at what seem to be rock-bottom prices. So far as line is concerned, especially nylon monofilament, the longer it is stored, especially if exposed to bright sunlight, the less suitable for fishing it becomes. Therefore such items offered under the heading 'Huge Stock Clearance' are always suspect. The line you purchase at such a bargain price may be nothing of the kind. It could be ancient, badly stored stock, which has so deteriorated that its stated breaking strain is now about double that of the figure it will snap at if put to a test.

Likewise, thousands of hooks at a give-away price do not suggest to the circumspect buyer that they are the product of a reputable maker. There is absolutely no point from a thrift aspect in stocking up with a huge quantity of any kind of fishing tackle—no matter how cheap—if it is of such inferior quality that you have no confidence in it when you use it, or if you foolishly buy such a huge quantity that there is not the slightest chance that you will use half of it even if you live to a ripe old age.

6
The Angler's Personal Equipment

A long time ago, when everyone seemed to be much poorer than they are today, there was no special clothing on the market which had been specifically created with the fisherman's comfort and protection in mind. Old working clothing was usually called into service as angling wear and it did a very poor job, letting in the rain and hail and becoming as heavy as lead when it got thoroughly saturated. Nowadays, however, the angler is in a happy position when it comes to choosing suitable apparel. Not only can he buy items which have been purpose-made for him; he can also look over a whole range of sailing, golfing, mountaineering, hiking and even potholing gear and often find something which is absolutely ideal from a comfort and weather-beating point of view when used on the shoreline. Moreover, the bigger fishing tackle shops often have what I choose to term an angler's sartorial elegance department – usually a special section set aside from the actual fishing tackle and devoted solely to creature comforts for the customer. Here the fisherman will find an angling wardrobe where everything from waterproof boots to deerstalker hats can be bought.

However, in view of the fact that the all-year-round shore fisherman (who also digs his own bait) pursues his activities in all weathers on a variety of fishing marks, some of which demand long walks and the agility of a mountain goat to reach them, a standard set of angling wear will not be suitable for all occasions. What is required is a selection of garments which are interchangeable. Footwear also comes into this same category. For instance, after digging bait in a pair of thigh boots in the middle of summer, it would be most uncomfortable to keep them on all day while fishing from a high, dry, smooth concrete pier.

To be quite candid, some of the factors which govern the duration of your fishing times and the locations you choose are age, your state of physical fitness, and whether you like to spice your outings with a dash of danger or prefer to be safe and secure the whole time. Senior citizens do not usually like to climb down precipitous rocks in the dark to fish for conger eels. Nor is it usual for young men full of boundless energy to sit warm and cosy on covered-in piers, drinking tea, smoking pipes and nodding off in between the tinklings of a rod end bell, which signal a bite.

When considering that most static of shore anglers, the pier, jetty or harbour wall fisherman who buys his bait and drives up in style to his fishing station in a car, which he parks close by, the clothing question is no problem. Since he is largely inactive except for sudden bouts of violent activity when he strikes, hooks and subsequently lands a whopper, he can cocoon himself in the heaviest and thickest gear imaginable without the slightest discomfort.

One great forward stride which has been made recently is the tightening up of the laws relating to advertising. The word 'waterproof' must now mean precisely what it says. It is amusing to find that certain garments, which previously carried such a label, have now had their descriptions considerably modified: 'water resistant' or even 'showerproof' is how the makers choose to describe them in order to enable their products to conform to the new regulations.

After digressing a little, let us now return to Mr Average Angler, standing on his local pier in the depths of winter with a great ball of shop-bought lugworm on his hook, waiting for a monster cod to take hold. From his birthday suit, working outwards in ever increasing layers, his angling wear could be as follows. First, a layer of thermal underwear – long johns and half-sleeved vest: amazingly warm, rather expensive, and must be carefully hand washed and dried. Failing such luxury, the poor man's second-best equivalent could be a string vest worn next to the skin, topped by the usual underwear and then a pair of winceyette pyjamas, over which is worn a normal shirt, trousers, heavy roll-necked sweater and a knee-length 100 per cent waterproof coat, with thick insulating lining and a draw-string hood. With this outfit I would suggest a pair of thigh boots, not because they are needed to keep out water but for the simple reason that if they are worn over thick, knee-length woollen seaboot stockings with thermal socks underneath and heavy trousers, they are the warmest foot, leg and thigh wear I know.

Incidentally, to be sure of an absolutely 'warm-as-toast' start to an angling session which may begin at 4 o'clock on a freezing winter's morning, go to bed the night before in your underwear and pyjamas, but do not take them off when your alarm clock calls you to your fishing trip. Slip out of bed smartly and don your other clothes directly on top of the warm ones you are already wearing. The warm layer of air which has been building up next to your skin during the night seems to last all day long.

Now for the trouble spots, those areas which seem to suffer most from the cold. I am referring, of course, to the extremities: feet and hands, and also the area around the head, neck and ears, which, even with a large turned-up collar, a scarf, and a hat with ear flaps, still seems to cause discomfort in a half gale on a windswept shoreline.

Beginning with the feet, always buy rubber boots and waders one size larger than you normally need in ordinary footwear; this will allow the space between foot and boot to be insulated effectively. I find that a pair of thick wool socks, with the addition of 'socketts' or 'footlets', will keep the feet dry and warm all day. The very latest PVC 'space boots' with insulated 'liners' are fantastic footwarmers for static anglers on freezing-footed concrete piers, but they are rather expensive and I do not recommend them for long, tiring walks over rough ground.

Hands are a special problem. Great thick leather gauntlet gloves or sheepskin lined mittens are wonderful, but how on earth do you handle your tackle with them on? And if you take them off and put them down on the harbour wall or the beach, they are sure to get blown into the water and end up washing around in the rising tide. Should you be extra careful and put them somewhere secure while you attend to your baiting-up chores, you will need to wash and dry your hands thoroughly before you put them on again. Otherwise, if you thrust wet smelly hands into them each time you handle anything which is the least bit pungent, the gloves will finally take on such a fish-dock aroma and be so cold and soggy inside that you will be quite happy if, the next time you take them off, a gust of wind does blow them into the sea.

The complete answer to this hand-warming problem is a small innovation of mine called 'sheepskin pockets'. When you buy an angling coat or jacket, make sure that it has two very roomy pockets – one at each side. Then measure them carefully and take yourself off to an arts and crafts shop which sells sheepskin offcuts cheap. You require enough to line each pocket, and the sheepskin is merely tacked into place with large stitches so that it can be taken out and washed at regular intervals when it becomes too smelly. Gloves then become superfluous. You have two built-in handwarmers – one on each side of your coat.

Now for that vital head and nape of the neck area, from which emanate stiffness, ills and chills if it is not cossetted properly. Hats, scarves and turned-up collars do a good job of keeping these parts reasonably warm, but they are no match for the icy blasts which sometimes whistle around on an exposed beach. Observe the eskimo dress style with the one piece fur-lined parka – no hat to blow off, hood and jacket all in one single garment, with a draw-cord round the neck and another round the hood. The whole affair can be snugged down to give sealed-off, effective warmth, which is the desired result.

Having dealt with cold-beating gear for the static pier angler, whose only energetic activity is a short walk from his car, carrying his tackle, to his chosen fishing position, we now approach a decidedly different type of angling enthusiast: the roving, wandering, rock-climbing angler, who also indulges in that most temperature-raising chore—bait digging. To save all newcomers to the sport a great deal of cash, and also to prevent them from spoiling good angling garments, I would say reserve your oldest clothes for this task and let them be of a kind which can easily be washed. Or, in the case of waterproof coats and trousers, they must be made of some material which will take kindly to a good washing down with a hose pipe because they will surely need it after they have been subjected to the rigours of a gooey mud-flat for three or four hours. At the risk of offending all those makers of garments which are claimed to 'breathe' and not cause inner condensation, I would suggest that, before they are labelled with such a glowing description, they should be tested out under actual 'battlefield' conditions by someone who is trying to dig lugworms in a hurry on a rapidly rising tide. In the past, I have experimented with all kinds of clothing for bait digging, in an attempt to overcome the 'Turkish bath' effect which strenuous exercise produces when the wearer is encased in waterproof clothing. To date I regret to report I have come nowhere near solving the problem, if it is raining heavily and you wish to dig bait without getting wet. By wearing all-enveloping waterproofs you will certainly prevent the rain from getting in; but, alas, your body will generate so much moisture inside your clothing (which is trapped and cannot escape) that you will most probably end up a darned sight wetter *inside* than *out*!

In all sincerity, the problem is insurmountable. You either dig in light clothing and get thoroughly soaked from outside by the weather, or put on all your rain-beating gear and end up just as wet—but from two sources, inside and out. Exactly the same conditions prevail if you have long walks or steep climbs to your angling station. If you put on a great pile of heavy clothing and perspire freely on your journey to the fishing, you will regret it as you stand clammy and shivering for perhaps five or six hours in a chilly wind. The secret is to carry your heavy clothes with you, preferably strapped to the top of a rucksack; do your walking in uncluttered comfort, and then put the extra layers of clothing on

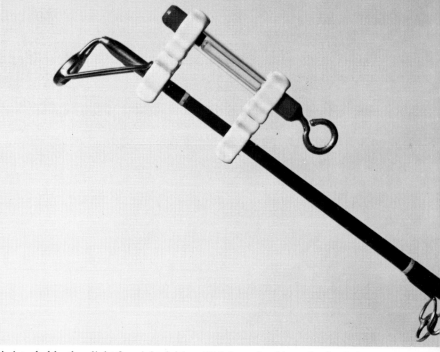

A detachable glow light for night fishing. This is preferable to the fixed tip light which is apt to cause snag-ups when casting in the dark

The carp fisher's 'Brolly-Camp'. It is adapted by sea anglers to make an easily transported and erected igloo shelter which can be set up well above the tide line

Gutting the catch at the end of a beach fishing session. A job to be done while the light is still good – but never with numb hands!

Classic example of the perfect lugworm cast, showing funnel at the head end and cast at the tail end

when you reach your angling destination.

One piece, zip-up, coverall angling suits, which encase the angler from ankles to the crown of his head, are becoming more popular every day; they completely obviate the need for separate jacket and trousers arrangements. These suits are available in various materials, qualities and styles. The cheapest, unlined suits are merely meant to act as an all-enveloping outer garment which should be worn with suitable warm clothing underneath. At the plushier end of the price bracket range, however, we find multi-zipped and press-studded garments which are guaranteed 100 per cent waterproof and suitable for extremely cold, even arctic, conditions. If your budget will stretch to the purchase of such 'Rolls Royce' angling apparel, by all means indulge yourself; for Siberian-style winter nights on exposed shorelines they are the last word in cosy comfort and waterproofing. Sweaters, scarves and padded trousers are completely redundant, if you are the proud possessor of such an article of angling wear. Wearing your normal indoor shirt and trousers, you can climb into your special angling suit and, after zipping and press-studding yourself securely inside, go out and face whatever the weather demons have in store for you, without a care in the world.

Unfortunately, although such one-piece angling suits are perfect in performance so far as warmth and protection are concerned, they have one great drawback which is not immediately apparent when you buy them. Briefly, they are an 'all or nothing' garment. Once you have put them on, you are committed to wearing them for the whole of your fishing session. Provided that the weather stays uniformly cold and wet, or just cold, your comfort is assured. However, in changeable weather conditions one-piece arctic suits can be trying. Perhaps you set out to fish an exposed beach on a cold November morning with a biting onshore wind blowing strongly right into your face. On goes your super-warm one-piece suit and you fish in sumptuous comfort until noon. But when the wind shifts round to blow strongly offshore, the temperature suddenly soars and the sun begins to shine. What a dilemma! If you divest yourself of your thick one-piece suit, the weather, although it has become warmer, is still not suitable for shirt-sleeves. Therefore you have the choice of keeping on your super suit and baking inside it, or doffing it and feeling distinctly chilly. In such circumstances, a spare sweater and a lightweight nylon anorak or cagoule, rolled up and carried on the top of your angling haversack or rucksack, would solve the problem.

Whilst on the subject of tackle carriers, bags, rucksacks and haversacks, let me point out the advantages and drawbacks of the different kinds so far as the sea fishing shore angler is concerned. First: the 'comfortable locations operators'. When fishing from a pier, jetty or harbour wall, a large, roomy tackle-carrier-cum-seat will prove satisfactory from a sitting-down and also tackle-and-bait-storage aspect. But for long shore walks, cliff slithering, and rock climbing, a back-packing type of tackle carrier is necessary in order to avoid shoreline accidents. Haversacks or tackle carriers with single-strap slings are 'sudden death' if you try to climb down steep rocks while carrying them. You may commence your climb with the tackle carrier located firmly in its correct position on your back; but, as you proceed, it may make a sudden unbalancing shift round to the front of your body with the sling becoming tangled with one of your arms. This is very unnerving and decidedly dangerous if you are negotiating a steep rock face above deep water. For such difficult terrain a rucksack with double shoulder harness and a waist belt is the only safe style for transporting your gear.

In view of the fact that, when shore fishing rods are dismantled into two pieces, their length is still a rather cumbersome five or six feet, it is a temptation, when shore wandering, to tie them to your back pack in order to leave both your hands free for climbing activities. This is a most unwise practice. Carry the rods and monopods or tripods in your hands; that way, you will at least be conscious of what you are doing with them. Strapped to your back, they are out of sight and out of mind; they can cause you to overbalance and fall heavily, should they catch on a protruding rock or become wedged in a crack and suddenly check your progress.

With all this talk of rock climbing and cliff scrambling coming up in almost every paragraph of this chapter, a survey of sensible, appropriate angling footwear is called for at this point. Most popular are rubber knee-length boots, which are available with either deep rubber treaded soles and heels or rubber soles and heels with overall steel studding to give greater grip on green, weed-covered rocks. I like knee-length rubber boots because they are easier to walk in than thigh waders, and they do not make the tops of your legs uncomfortably hot in summer. Unfortunately, however, whenever I wear knee-length boots I invariably get a 'boot full' almost every time I am fishing, especially if I am on a beach with running surf. The reason is that I seem incapable of judging exactly, when I am wading in a short distance to cast, how deep the water is and where on my legs the next advancing wave will reach. All very off-putting, if you are careless and get the sea coming over the top of both boots!

Thigh boots or waders are my favourite shore fishing wear, and these also are produced with either rubber treaded or steel studded soles. For the rough and tumble of shore fishing and rock scrambling, however, I do not advise the use of waders of the ultra-lightweight fly fisher's type. Barnacle-covered rocks soon rip them to pieces or cause the legs to leak.

Breast-high or chest waders, which have been 'purloined' by shorecasters from the salmon fishing scene, are the ultimate in surf fishing wear. They are really marvellous for deep wading on flat, sandy storm-beaches when fishing for bass in the long, regular 'water tables'. They are also very warm for fishing on exposed shorelines, as they can be worn with just a short jacket or smock over them, which dispenses completely with knee or thigh boots and waterproof trousers. But the angler must always limit himself to safe shore fishing situations if he wishes to avoid accidents when he is wearing them. Level shorelines, with regular water surf-tables, are the ideal places for deep surf wading and very little can go wrong in such circumstances, apart from the fisherman being foolish and venturing out too far and getting bowled over by an extra big wave. On no account chance your arm by deep wading on an irregular beach or shore with rocky gullies and small raised sandbanks. No matter how careful you are in keeping your line of retreat firmly fixed in your mind's eye you will eventually come unstuck. If you are fortunate, you could merely suffer an overall wetting and the loss of your tackle. If the worst happens, however, you will figure as one of the many victims which the sea claims each year.

For the ascent and descent of rock marks and when fishing on green, weed-covered rock platforms, I am never completely happy unless I am wearing real climbing boots with lots of steel studs in the soles and heels to give me an absolutely sure-footed grip. Unfortunately, in such shore fishing situations, if there are rocky pools everywhere and the occasional wave sends a gush of water round the angler's feet, his leather boots, although keeping him from slipping, will not also ensure that he is dryfooted. This is a difficult problem which can only be solved by the use of strap-on rock spikes. These are light steel footpieces which have toe and ankle straps and projecting metal teeth, which will very effectively bite deep down into thick kelp or green slimy weed and give the angler the most secure footing it is possible to have. One great advantage of these strap-on rock spikes is their lightness and the ease with which they can be carried around at the bottom of your rucksack. A long walk can be done to a remote rock mark in rubber knee boots, if the approach is through shallow pools and over tracts of sploshy mud; then, when a secure, non-slip foot grip is required, the rock spikes can be conveniently strapped to the angler's feet.

Many more pairs of thigh boots and chest waders are ruined by being wrongly stored than are actually worn out by long usage. If you carelessly dump this kind of angling wear in a heap on the garage floor on your return from a fishing trip, watch out for cracking and leaks around the knee sections the next time you wear them. The only way to store waders or thigh boots is to hang them upside down so that the tops do not fold over and weaken the material where it is bent in one position for perhaps weeks or, in some cases, even months.

As waders and thigh boots are quite expensive, it is a wise and thrifty move to buy a pair of specially designed wader clasps which are used to suspend the waders upside down. They then hang straight and, also of great importance, any water in them drains out and they are subject to a free circulation of air which prevents mildew and rotting attacking the inner lining. To save expense, a very efficient wader and thigh boot storage unit can be constructed by nailing broad stretchy upholstery webbing with large-headed carpet tacks to a plank, so that several pairs of loops are formed. The plank or board is then secured with brackets lengthwise at right angles to a wall in the garage or tackle store-room. With the loops facing downwards, the boots or wader toes are then pushed between the wood and the upholstery webbing loops, where they will hang securely in the approved upside-down position recommended by the makers.

To dry out waders or thigh boots quickly if they are very wet inside and they are needed urgently the next day, they should be correctly hung upside-down a few feet above an electric fan heater which is directed upwards towards their open tops.

If your financial situation is rosy and your tastes run to purpose-designed, high-class angling wear, by all means indulge your fancy and march down to the shoreline looking like a genuine 22-carat angler who has just stepped off the front cover of a sporting magazine. Looking the part will certainly boost your ego and give you the confidence to feel quite sure that the fish are just queueing up to sample your bait. But for the budget-clothing buyers, whose cash flow may not be so good, there are lots of economy avenues which can be explored. For instance, fish dock workers need to be clad in almost the same style as beach fishers, especially if they are working outdoors all the year round. Although the clothes they wear to keep themselves dry and warm may not be as brightly coloured or as well cut as the best quality tackle catalogue stuff, they are at least functional and above all quite cheap. Ship chandlers, fishermen's clothing stores, and industrial garment suppliers are the sources from which bargain-price angling clothing can be obtained—not forgetting the government-surplus merchants.

One comforting item which I must describe in some detail is the Brolly-Camp, the waterproof cover which fits right over the traditional fisherman's umbrella when it is erected and magically transforms it into a completely rain- and wind-proof igloo. This has been 'adopted' from the carp-fishing fraternity by a number of beach anglers who fish at locations where a steep-to beach with a nearby grassy bank enables them to erect what I will call a base-camp-shelter.

For some years now the large, green traditional angling umbrella has been used on some shorelines by sea anglers, especially the paraffin pressure lamp brigade who find that a large 'brolly' anchored well down makes a marvellous windbeater. Recently the all-night and weekend camping type of anglers have discovered that the canvas Brolly-Camp is without a doubt the most easily transported and erected instant shelter they have ever used. In drab olive green or a camouflage pattern, it blends well with the shoreline landscape and does not offend the eye of anyone whose pet aversion is coastal campers. If it is used wisely in a responsible manner on shores where the local byelaws do not forbid such activities, it can in times of very adverse weather conditions transform what would have been a miserable rain-soaked outdoor fishing marathon into a session which was quite enjoyable because the anglers had somewhere in which to shelter to escape the worst of the weather.

One final point; I am sure many anglers have become infuriated, when digging bait and crouching low over their forks, to find that their modern short-length shirts ride right up their backs and leave that vital lumbago area exposed to the chilly shoreline blast. No longer will such a problem trouble you if you look through the advertising pages of the angling press. There you will find listed a special long-tailed angler's shirt which is guaranteed to stay firmly tucked in.

7
All About Bait

The digging, catching or gathering of bait is viewed by some sea anglers as a muscle-straining, back-breaking chore, which is best avoided if alternative means are readily available (unlimited cash for instance) to obtain it the easy way. But there is no other method of learning about fish and their feeding habits which will surpass the knowledge gained down on the shoreline seeking out the food upon which fish exist. In addition, if your bait-gathering ground is also the same stretch of beach, rock mark or mudflat over which you will later cast your tackle when fishing, then your chances, if you have been observant, of locating and catching the species you are after are exceedingly high. Many times better in fact than those of the casual angler with the shop-bought bait, who wanders down to the shoreline at high tide when all the natural geographical features of the beach are covered by water, and hopefully fishes 'blind', casting his tackle out to some spot which he hopes may hold a fish or two.

Without a doubt, lugworms are our most widely used and easily located sea fishing bait. Their characteristic funnel and worm cast indications can be found almost everywhere around the British Isles on sand, mud and a mixture of both. The best worm colonies flourish where there is a gentle run of tide and no violent wave action to churn up the worm beds. There will never be a nation-wide shortage of lugworms, as some pessimists predict; only a local shortage, because of senseless over-digging on some well-known bait beds. In certain remote parts of Scotland I have motored along whole stretches of quiet estuarial shorelines with rich lugworm beds running for mile after mile – and never a digger in sight.

All very fine, you may say, to regale us with such tales. But how does the tyro sea angler go about getting himself a bucketfull of such wonderful bait? The first wise move is to locate the nearest 'diggings' and, choosing a time when the tide is well down, go and watch the experts at work. You will learn more in half a day there, if you keep your eyes open and are observant, than I could teach you in a book twice the size of this one.

The first thing to note is what type of digging tool is being used: 'spud' fork, three-tined, long-handled fork, or 'grafter' spade. Next pay careful attention to the kind of worms which are coming out: big, thick black ones, or smaller thinner red worms. Finally, note carefully the digging method which is being used. Are the fork or spade operators digging single 'blow holes' and 'worm casts', to unearth one worm at a time? Or are they 'trenching' in allotment digging style and forking out several worms with each two or three insertions of the tool? On some very sploshy, mud-flat shorelines where the water does not drain off, you will see the squeegee method being used. Briefly, a 3 or 4ft-wide rubber-bladed squeegee is used to remove the surface water and throw up a low 6in wall of mud, in a square, round the chosen digging area. Then the dried out surface can be dug for the worms without the holes filling up with water, which prevents the worms being easily located.

Worm digging is hard, dirty work, especially if the bait bed is gooey mud and the walk to and from it is long. But the more remote the bait beds are and the harder the worms are to dig, the fewer professionals you will find there. The private angler/digger requiring fifty or a hundred worms for himself can afford to dig for large, good quality worms and take his time, whereas the man doing the job for a living must get so many hundred worms and nearly always watch the tide and dig against the clock.

Store your lugworms in plastic or wooden containers and segregate the damaged ones from those which are sound and whole. Wash them in clean sea water before you leave the shoreline and then let them drain off on sheets of dry newspaper on a cool concrete floor. Worms for immediate use can be carried to the shoreline wrapped in packs of twenty in flat, newspaper parcels. Short-term storage is possible by either leaving the live worms in a cool location (a concrete garage floor) on sea water-dampened sacking well away from the sunlight, or storing the flat, newspaper parcels with a score of worms in each in the salad crisper compartment of a household refrigerator.

In recent years great strides have been made in the direction of permanent lugworm aquarium storage in salt water with air pump aeration. Provided they are segregated into separate compartments in the same aquarium, ragworms and peeler crabs can also be kept for long periods in this manner. In the interests of economy, it is not even necessary to go to the expense of buying a specially constructed glass tank. Plastic dustbins and water tanks will serve the purpose of 'wormariums' just as well.

Temperature control is vital when storing live sea baits in this manner. If the tank is wrongly situated so that it receives direct warmth from hot summer sun, then goodbye to your fresh live bait – and the smell of the corpses will be appalling. Choose a cool location away from the warming effect of sunlight and keep the water temperature in the 35° to 45°F range.

The angler who digs lugworms will invariably turn up with his fork a cream-coloured centipede-like creature, the white ragworm, which, incidentally, should be housed in a separate bait container and not mixed with the lugworms. There are four distinct types of ragworms to be found on our shorelines: the white rag already mentioned; the small red harbour ragworm, beloved bait of young boys who delight in grovelling in the mud for it and becoming disgustingly filthy; the red ragworms of the shoreline which can reach a size of 6in; and last, but of great importance baitwise, the giant king ragworm, a fearsome green-coloured marine borer which is found in the extreme lower littoral zone. This is a worm which can attain and exceed the 2ft mark, and it is also notable for a pair of nippers in its head which can draw blood if the bait digger is careless in handling it.

All the ragworm family are lovers of mud, and they thrive best of all in a mixture of estuarial mud, sand and finely ground shell. As they do not leave the characteristic blow hole and cast of the lugworm, they are rather difficult for the inexperienced bait digger to locate until he becomes skilled at winkling them out of their natural habitat. Very low spring tides, which uncover the extremity of the littoral zone, provide the best king ragworm digging conditions. A rather light 'pussy-footed' tread is necessary to locate the ragworm, as small water spouts will shoot up from the sand when the worm in its burrow feels pressure from the digger's footfalls. Immediately a burrow is located, a forkful of the sand and mud mixture is quickly taken out so that the downward 'hole' can be followed and excavated. Some ragworms lie very deep and it is often necessary to go down to a depth of 2 or 3ft to finally extract the worm. It is a matter of personal preference which tool is used. A fork will uncover a large area very quickly if the worms are so numerous that they can be 'trench' dug and picked out with every forkful, while a narrow bladed spade of the 'grafter' type will enable the digger to follow the burrows of the extremely large deep-boring worms and get them out without a lot of strenuous earth moving being done.

Ragworms are best stored in a lidded bait box, with each type kept separate. Put a layer of damp sand at the bottom and a quantity of wet seaweed on the top, so that the worms will not dehydrate and die off quickly. Like lugworms, ragworms cannot stand extreme temperatures – either too hot or too cold. Kept in wet sand and seaweed, they will remain in good condition for up to a week or even ten days, provided the bait box is kept in a cool, dark place. A regular inspection of the live stock of worms is vital so that any that are dead, sickly or ailing can be removed.

For long-term marine tank storage it is necessary that ragworms are not kept in separate perforated containers. Although lugworms and most other sea baits will survive in this manner, the ragworms seem to prefer a free swimming mode of existence. Cover the bottom of the marine tank with three or four inches of sand and small shingle and make sure that there is adequate aeration from the electric pump. When introducing the worms into this environment, make sure that every worm is alive and flourishing; dead worms can easily be spotted because they will lie inert instead of wriggling away to hide themselves. As with bait box storage, each type of ragworm should be housed separately because of their cannibalistic tendencies if mixed together.

As regards shellfish baits, I cannot understand why the mussel is so popular as a sea fishing bait on the North East coast—both with sport anglers and commercial longliners—and yet is sadly neglected and sometimes apparently unknown away from this area. As a cheap and easily obtained bait the mussel is definitely in a class on its own; perhaps that is the reason why it is not used on a wide scale. It may be that the majority of sea anglers are conditioned to high shop prices or great inconvenience before they consider a bait worth a trial. Since mussels are found almost everywhere around the coast, near the low tidal zone, the thrifty angler will have no difficulty in pulling off great bunches and filling a bucket with them in a few minutes. Those about 3in long are the best size for bait.

To keep them alive and in perfect condition store them in fresh sea water in a large container in a cool place and feed them a small quantity of fine, crushed oats which will fatten them up enormously. Although the collecting and storage of mussels is easy, I think the extraction of them for bait is what deters the average sea angler from using them on his hook. Their resistance to being extracted from their shells causes more cut fingers and lost tempers than any other sea angling bait operation I know. The golden rule for safe mussel opening is: a short-bladed sharp knife and unlimited patience. Knack and knowhow are the secret watchwords to successful mussel opening. To see an East coast bait operator steadily work his way through a hundredweight sack of mussels, whilst talking and apparently paying no regard to what he is doing with his hands, is indeed an angling education.

There are numerous, very quick ways to open mussels. And

the experts make it look so simple, it is not to be wondered at that the eager amateur tries to emulate their speed and style and cuts himself badly. An ordinary bone-handled table knife makes a very good mussel-extracting tool after it has been suitably modified. The blade, which should be thin and fairly 'bendy', should be shortened until it is just a couple of inches long. Then a keen edge should be ground on it both sides and on the rounded point as well. The object of having a very short blade is to allow the knife hand to work very close to the mussel so that absolute control can be exercised over the knife movements.

When making a first attempt to open mussels, almost everyone approaches the job in the identical wrong way. They foolishly hold the mussel tightly in their clenched palm, aim a sharp-pointed, long-bladed knife at the slit in the twin shells and give an impatient thrust. Naturally, the knife point slips off the hard, shiny surface of the rounded mussel shell and drives deep into the palm of the hand holding it – all very painful and offputting. As I stressed earlier: don't rush the mussel opening and everything will turn out as planned.

The first job is to take a good look at a live mussel and closely observe how it is formed. It consists of two convex shells, hinged together at the sharp end on the curved side. If you work right handed – by that I mean with the knife in the right hand – take the mussel in the left hand and hold it between the forefinger and thumb with the pointed end to the left and the straight side of the mussel nearest your body. Now apply gentle opposite pressure to the convex shells, with finger and thumb, pushing away with the thumb and pulling towards you with the tip of the forefinger. When you exert the correct amount of pressure the top shell slides just a little way out of line from the bottom shell, forming a slight lip on the curved side of the mussel with the top shell slightly overhanging the bottom one. That is the precise spot at which the rounded point of the thin bladed knife is inserted in an angled upward direction to enter the mussel shell quite easily and safely.

Once the point of the knife is into the mussel between the two halves of the shell, the hardest part of the job has been accomplished. Keep a firm hold on the mussel with the left finger and thumb and gently slide the knife point all round the top shell in a clockwise direction. This will immediately release the bond of mussel flesh to the shell and enable the top half of the shell to be swung upwards quite easily on its hinge. Once this stage has been reached, the rest of the mussel extraction is simple; all the mussel operator has to do is to carefully scoop out the whole mussel from the bottom half of the shell by a circular motion of the knife.

If you proceed carefully in the manner outlined you will open your mussel without even a small nick on your hands and fingers. Also of paramount importance, the mussel will come out in one whole, presentable piece which will make a good hookbait. Don't ever be tempted to open your mussels in the lazy man's fashion by killing them off with hot water. This rough and ready treatment certainly ensures that the mussels come open and are easily extracted, because when the mussel expires its shell halves spring apart automatically. But by killing the mussel in this fashion you have destroyed all its natural attraction. The juices in its shell are vital to make the bait attractive and hot water destroys all the fishy smell appeal. Rather like taking a beautifully cooked lunch and putting it through an automatic washing machine before serving it!

To keep this essential mussel juice intact, store the shelled mussels in a screw-topped plastic container with the mussels floating in their own juice until they are needed for hookbait. On the East coast we find they are a superb cod bait if used in conjunction with lugworm as a lug and mussel cocktail. Half a dozen mussels are mounted on a large 6/0 long shanked hook and bound in place with a wrapping of weak 'rotten cotton'; then the whole delicious, succulent offering is tipped on the hook point with the thick head end of a juicy black lugworm.

To hook mussels correctly, so that they are tight on the hook shank and do not dangle around and fly off during casting, it is essential to put the hook point first through the central black or brown tongue of the mussel; then give the whole of the mussel a half twist and finish off by impaling it through the two gristly studs so that it is well secured. As mussel bait is considered most effective over weed and rock bottoms and lugworms are the bait to be used, appropriately enough, over where they are found – sand or mud – by using a mussel and lugworm cocktail the angler gets the best of both worlds so far as the attractiveness of his bait is concerned if he is fishing over a mixture of rock, weed, mud and sand.

Another very good cod and bass bait, which will take plaice and flounders as well, is that unmistakeable denizen of the seashore, the razorfish. Like the king ragworm, it inhabits the lower littoral zone and is best obtained on the low water mark at the bottom of the big fortnightly Spring tides. A casual beach walker would hardly realise that the razorfish were there under his feet unless one happened to appear above the surface of the sand. Sharp eyes and lightning reflexes are necessary if the razorfish hunter is to be successful in securing a good bait container-full of this very worthwhile hook offering. Incidentally, it can be deep frozen straight from the sea in its shell; it will keep indefinitely and when thawed out will make a most succulent and fairly tough hookbait, which will easily withstand the rigours of long casting without flying off the hook.

Although there are four separate species of razorfish found around the coast, the largest and most popular from a bait point of view is the pod razor, which can reach a length of up to 8in. Razorfish are vertical sand borers and have syphons at the end which is uppermost in the sand; these give the tell-tale squirts by which the bait catcher spots his prey. At the other end of the shell is a powerful muscular 'foot' which is extended down into the sand, enabling the razorfish to grip and pull down its shell with amazing speed and strength.

It can take an amateur bait gatherer quite some time to acquire the knack of being able to spot the presence of razorfish. The easiest way I know to learn it is to walk backwards on the water's edge of a low Spring tide in a sheltered area, which has no pounding wave action and a shoreline of fine gently shelving sand. There is method in this walking backwards madness. If you walk in a forward direction what you will not see is the small spouts of the razorfish, for the precise reason that, as you pass over it and the razor feels your foot vibrations, it squirts its jets of water upwards and uses its 'foot' to slide quickly down into its burrow. By walking backwards, your eyes can follow your line of retreat very closely and immediately spot the razor squirts, or, if there are no jets of water, you will at least see a small keyhole-shaped depression which appears in the surface of the sand as the razorfish makes its downward journey to escape.

Now, having discovered how to locate your razorfish, the next rather tricky task is how to get it out – in one undamaged piece and in sufficient quantities to make razorfish hunting a worthwhile bait-gathering pursuit. There are three popular methods of extracting the razors from their sandy habitat: digging, salting and spearing. Of the three, I find spearing the most difficult to learn, salting the best for obtaining the bait absolutely undamaged, and digging the least effective and definitely the most destructive of the bait, unless the operator is possessed of lightning reflexes, hawk eyes and a finely developed sixth sense which guides his spadework.

To dig razorfish I use a three-tined sandworm fork or a narrow-bladed 'grafter' spade. Quickness is vital. The object is to get the fork below the razorfish while it is near the surface, and with great manual dexterity quickly flip it out of its sandy burrow before it can retreat deep down into the seashore. With a spade, it is necessary first to locate the razor near the surface; then, judge its depth and, with a lightning thrust of the spade, block off its retreat. All much easier said than done! The learner will damage lots of razorfish and only get a few out of the sand unbroken.

The second method, salting, would at first sound almost unbelievable. The 'tools' required are a canister of ordinary household salt with a pouring lip and a discarded washing-up liquid squirter bottle filled with sea water. If you feel at all unsure of this method and do not wish to appear on the shoreline looking like someone who is off his rocker with salt and squeezy bottle, squirting it into holes in the sand, choose a very remote beach until you find to your amazement that the method is a sure-fire way to extract undamaged razors. Briefly, the 'salt-and-squeezy' *modus operandi* goes like this. First find your razor hole and make sure a fish is in residence. Next, tip a little salt down the hole and follow it up with a squirt of sea water. What happens next is truly fantastic. Up pops the razorfish sometimes almost totally out of the sand so that it is able to be grasped and firmly withdrawn. But never be impatient with this razor catching technique. If you try to take the razorfish between your finger and thumb just as it is emerging, it will take fright and realise what is happening; then, before you can get it extracted, down it will go, because there is not enough of it above the sand to ensure a firm grip on it. Various theories have been advanced as to why salty water causes the razorfish to emerge. One idea is that the razor is irritated into emerging by the salt. Another school of thought suggests that the salty water convinces the razorfish that the tide is flooding in over it and it is safe to emerge. Right or wrong, what does it matter? So long as the method of extraction works – and believe me it does – I do not spend too much thought on razorfish psychology.

The spearing of razorfish is definitely a delicate art which is not learned overnight. First the 'spear': this can be fashioned quite easily by a DIY enthusiast. All that is required is a 2 or 3ft length of round, mild steel rod which is then rubbed with emery cloth until it is absolutely smooth and burnished. There is a vitally important reason for this polishing process which will be revealed later.

At one end of the steel rod a double spearhead barb must be formed by heating up the metal, flattening it, filing, and then re-tempering it. This barbed spearhead should be kept quite small and neat, only a little larger in diameter than the steel shaft, in fact. For efficiency it is essential that no handle is put on the razor spear; in use it is wrapped at the end opposite to the barbed point with a strip of coarse towelling which will prevent the

For mudflat worm digging a broad tined 'spud' fork will winkle out the lugworms better than a traditional worm fork. Safety note: never venture out onto extensive tracts of shoreline without a reliable compass and a good knowledge of your directions

Thick, juicy, 8in mudflat lugworms. Bait *par excellence* for winter cod fishing, but the Devil's own job to procure

A sharp eyed assistant to pick up the worms will make the task of lugworm digging much easier

When worm casts are as numerous as these a trenching method of digging can be employed. Note the darker casts, which are from very deep boring 'gully' lugworms well down in the black ooze

metal from damaging the operator's palm.

How to use it is the next delicate problem! As with salting, first locate your razorfish in its sandy burrow. Observe the angle of the hole carefully to make sure what alignment it takes; it may not go absolutely vertically into the sand. Now for the all-important insertion of the home-made, shiny steel, ¼in diameter spear. Insert the spear in the direction that the hole would seem to take and with one hand on the towelling wrapping to give the necessary thrust and the other guiding the spear into the hole, gently 'probe' in a downward direction, trying to feel what is happening to the spear point. If you have done the job properly, on its way down the spear point will grate on the edge of the razorfish shell and then enter it, when you will feel a slight resistance as it penetrates the razorfish flesh. At this stage of the proceedings, it is necessary to push down a further six inches or so until it is estimated that the razorfish spear has passed right down the shell and is protruding from the bottom. Give the spear a half-turn to lock the barbs in the shell and gently withdraw it, with the razorfish, we hope, firmly impaled on the end of it.

At this point you will find out why there should be no fixed handle on the spear and why it should be smooth and shiny. Unwrap the towelling from the end of the spear and gently slide the razorfish up and off the spear. If the spear had been made with a fixed wooden handle the razorfish would be badly damaged as the bait operator attempted to pull it off the double barbed point—rather like trying to get a deeply embedded hook out of your flesh by brute force.

In addition to mussels and razorfish, which are the two most popular and easily obtained shellfish hook offerings for the shore angler to use, there are quite a number of other shell-dwelling sea creatures which make very good baits. Whelks are a very tough bait, much favoured by commercial long-line fishermen because of their ability to stay on the hook in rough weather and withstand the nibbling of crabs and small fish. So far as the shore angler is concerned, the whelk is certainly a bait which will stand up to hard casting without being ripped from the hook. It is no use attacking the whelk in its shell with a knife; the only way to extricate it is to break open the shell with a hammer.

Cockles are a rather small bait, which is often neglected by the majority of anglers who think that bait size is of paramount importance. Cockles can be raked with an ordinary garden rake from sandy, and sometimes muddy, shorelines, usually in sheltered locations away from strong tidal flows. Your special mussel knife will open cockle shells easily, if they are rested on a piece of wood with the hinged part downward and the knife blade is inserted from the open side and pressed firmly until both halves of the shell are prised open. Hold the cockle firmly between finger and thumb on the board and keep the knife under control all the time to avoid gashed fingers.

When digging bait, especially lugworms, in locations that are muddy, the angling bait seeker will often unearth clams or, as the Americans call them, 'gapers'. These shellfish are easily captured as, unlike the razorfish, they cannot make a rapid escape downwards deeper into the sand. Opening clams is done in much the same way as mussels. A thin knife blade is inserted between the shells at a point away from the hinge and the blade gently worked round the separate halves to cut the 'meat' from the shells.

The slipper limpet is a shell dweller which is more often 'beachcombed' after a storm rather than gathered by design. This is because its natural habitat is that part of the shoreline which is usually beneath the waves at all states of the tide. Slipper limpets will usually be found in numbers, all mounted 'pick-a-back' style, one on top of the other. Prize them apart with a strong knife blade and extract them by running the knife point round inside the shell.

If on your bait-questing forays along the shoreline, especially in areas of chalky cliffs or where soft limestone rocks abound, you chance to see someone operating down near the waterline with a hammer and chisel, observe him carefully. At first you may be under the impression that you are witnessing a geologist at work. Look even closer and engage him in conversation. You will find that he is a bait-seeking angler after a bivalve mollusc called the common piddock, which is a rock-borer. I find that the rather novel pursuit of piddocks is quite amusing for the first-time bait collector who has never seen how it is done before. When a burrow is located, I usually ask the person assisting me to peer in closely to see if the piddock is at home, and then tap the rock gently with his hammer. Without fail, if the burrow is occupied, the prospecting bait seeker gets a jet of water in his face which denotes that the piddock is in residence and trying to retreat further into its hiding place. A little careful hammer and chisel work will soon extract the piddock, which must be handled with care as its shell is quite thin and decidedly brittle.

Sandeels are a much sought after bait, especially in the West Country around the Cornwall area. They are seine netted professionally and sold both as live bait, fresh from the sea, and in packs after they have been rapidly blast frozen. There are two distinct species of sandeel which come into the shallows around our shorelines: the lesser sandeel, which is the one most bait seekers come into contact with when forking over wet sand for lugworms, and the greater sandeel or launce which can grow to a size of 18in.

Sandeels prefer a bottom of coarse sand with a good tidal flow over it to oxygenate the water. There are various methods for taking sandeels, some of which demand much more skill and manual dexterity than others. Digging is quite the most popular method used by anglers. As they invariably find themselves down on the shoreline with a lugworm fork and plenty of time to kill before their favourite low-water lugworm beds are uncovered, it is natural that they are apt to fill in the waiting period with a sandeel hunt. Although on really productive ground it is quite easy to turn up goodly quantities of sandeels with your fork, getting your hands on them quick enough to capture them before they literally melt away before your eyes is a different matter. A two-man (four-handed) team makes the best working combination, one forking the sand over and the other crouching low ready to grab the little blighters before they vanish in a flash.

'Scraping' or 'hooking' for sandeels is definitely an expert's method, but it can easily be learned by anyone who is willing to watch it being done and then practise hard with the right tool until the necessary skill is obtained. I have seen sandeel 'hooks' made up from all kinds of weird and wonderful pieces of metal, from stiff, broad hacksaw blades and butchers' knives to the blades of old rusty sickles. Basically the 'launce' hook, as it is called, is a 12in blade with a handle at one end and a hook at the other. There is no cutting edge on the blade, but some sandeel experts do have a series of notches filed in the edge of the blade on the same side as the hook.

'Scraping' for sandeels is a shallow water catching method which will rapidly sort out the 'back-sufferers', as it is done in a crouching posture. To locate and take the sandeels, the bait hunter wades into the shallows and proceeds to slice the hook horizontally through the sand with a gentle figure of eight motion. All the while he maintains the free hand in a position just near the hook, above the surface of the water, so that when an eel is felt sliding along the blade it can rapidly be thrust into the water to trap the catch against the hook. Then both eel and hook are lifted from the water.

An extremely effective and decidedly lazy man's method of taking sandeels is the fork and push net technique – again a two-man operation. After locating a shallow run of water in which the sandeels are known to be, the fork operator walks in front and disturbs the eels from the sandy bottom so that they are washed into the push net as its operator follows close behind.

To keep sandeels alive and fresh, the shore fisherman can employ a small bait bucket and a battery-driven aerator, which can easily be carried around by him on his journey to the fishing mark. For long storage of large quantities of sandeels the marine aquarium set-up is recommended. A good shorefishing friend of mine, who is an absolute live-bait fanatic, has so many tanks and plastic buckets in his garage all bubbling away with various aerators fixed up to a special electric switchboard that there is no room for his new car. It languishes outside in the rain and

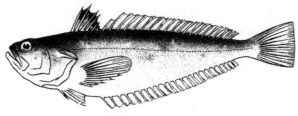
Lesser weever

mist – giving him endless starting problems all winter!

Whilst on the subject of wading in the shallows and groping around in the water with your hands to take sandeels, let me issue a very solemn warning regarding our only poisonous fish: the greater and lesser weevers. Make no mistake about it, I am not trying to be melodramatic when I say that the sting of the lesser weever is not something to be shrugged off, like the sting of a bee or a wasp. Weever stings need immediate hospital treatment to alleviate the dreadful pain which they cause. I witnessed the sad case of one angler with a weever sting in his palm, whose whole hand and arm swelled to such an alarming size that his jacket and shirt had literally to be cut off. He was delirious with the pain and screaming in the hospital casualty department to have his arm amputated immediately!

So far as the greater weever is concerned, the shore angler can happily dismiss it from his mind as it is usually found in deep water and is taken by boat anglers. However, the lesser weever will be found in the shallows in hot weather when a series of neap tides and calm weather provide the ideal warm water which it prefers. It is an unmistakeable fish about 4 to 6in in length with a short tapering yellowish-brown body and a large head with a pugnacious jaw and a gaping, uptilted mouth. The venomous spines are to be found on the first black dorsal fin (which the fish erects as it lies buried in the sand) and one on each gill cover. The truly diabolical aspect of the weevers is that their stings are capable of working long after the fish is dead.

To combat the weever fish menace effectively, and also to prevent your feet being lacerated by the many broken bottles which litter almost every beach, no matter how remote, the bare-footed and naked-handed approach to all things appertaining to shore wandering and bait catching must sadly be abandoned. Feet are easily protected by the wearing of rubber boots or light canvas shoes if the weather is exceptionally warm, but hands are a different problem. To be absolutely free from the weever sting hazard, always wear a thick pair of industrial type gloves for grubbing about on the shoreline when bait collecting or catching. And of vital importance, when shrimping and prawning with nets which often become clogged with weed, always carry an old well sharpened two-tined pickle fork to scrape over the catch and use it to spear the weever fish so that they are killed instantly. But on no account flick them off the fork so that they lie about the beach where they are just as capable of stinging when dead, as when they were alive. The sensible thing to do with dead weevers is to put them carefully into a separate bait box and preferably tip them into a fiery furnace when you arrive home – surely a fitting end for such an obnoxious pest.

One last word on this most unpleasant subject. If you should get stung – but I sincerely hope after reading this warning that you don't – squeeze the part round the sting very hard to raise it up and suck out the venom as hard as you can and then spit it out. This is the method that the East coast commercial fishermen use and it must be effective, as I have not yet heard of one losing a day's work by upping anchor after a weever sting and making a rapid return voyage for hospital treatment.

Prawns and shrimps are a particularly good live hook offering, especially when they are presented on light float tackle. This is an area of sea fishing bait where it is most advantageous if the angler lives near the coast, as such bait is not generally available through tackle shops. Live shrimps can easily be obtained by working the shallows over sand with a home-made push net. Such a net can be constructed quite simply from one of the modern onion sacks, which are made of nylon and are extremely strong and long-lasting. When designing a shrimp net which is to be purpose-made with nylon mesh and a collapsible push bar so that the whole affair can be folded up for easy transportation, always err on the small side. A great big net will certainly catch a load of shrimps and, as an added bonus, plenty of flatfish and the odd much relished sole at times. But push netting is very hard work and it is foolhardy to turn yourself into a semi-commercial slave, catching shrimps by the bucket-full, if it is really your intention to catch only as much bait as is necessary for a fishing trip.

So far as those top class bass baits—live prawns—are concerned, I have always found that, no matter how hard I try, I can never take too many. Some successful prawners boast that they eat whatever prawns are left over from a fishing trip. Unlike them, I regard this bait as so valuable—fishwise—that I consider it sacrilege to use it for human consumption.

Prawn hunting with a hand net on a shoreline which has many rocky pools is pure schoolboy magic on a hot day, and as an adult I enjoy it immensely—almost as much as fishing with them. The best prawn pools are those with a good depth of clear water and plenty of large rocks with 'curtains' of weed hanging from them; this is where the prawns will be hiding, right in among the weed, completely out of sight. The net, which should have a strong metal frame and a stout wooden handle, should be very thoroughly worked around all those densely weeded rocks with a scraping motion which will disturb the prawns and ensure that they are trapped in the meshes as the net is lifted to the surface. This type of prawn catching is rather slow and the prawns are usually captured in one and twos.

Drop netting is a technique which usually brings more prawns if several drop nets are available. It also has the advantage that the angler has no need to enter the water to work his nets—a decided 'plus' factor if the weather is rather chilly. Basically, this method of taking prawns closely resembles crayfish netting in fresh water. Two vital points to note are that a large cork should be fixed at the end of the three net-supporting ropes, and that the bait should not be tied to the bottom of the net but suspended across the top from a piece of cord fixed from one side to the

97

other. The reasons for these two ways of operating the drop net are as follows.

The cork supports the three ropes under the water and keeps them clear of the mouth of the net. Without it the ropes would lie across the mouth and when the net was pulled up they would lift off and allow any prawns which were resting upon them to escape. If the bait is tied in the bottom of the net, it is quite often smothered by it as it folds down on to the sand and, although the prawns may be attracted by it, they cannot settle down to feed upon it as they can if it is suspended in the middle of the net hoop.

All kinds of gruesome offerings can be used as bait for prawns, which are confirmed scavengers. Fish heads are very popular, but I have yet to find anything capable of attracting prawns so effectively as a very high kipper; perhaps it is the bright bronze dye or alternatively the oily herring flesh which they seem to find absolutely irresistible.

One other method of taking shrimps, and prawns as well, is 'scrape netting' along harbour walls which have a luxurious growth of thick weed. A small dinghy is necessary for this method of bait catching and the net used should be the flat fronted 'D'-shaped one. It is necessary to operate this technique when everything is quiet and a gentle neap tide is just lapping up to the harbour wall. Paddle the boat, without undue commotion, close to the weedy stonework and gently lower the net into the water and scrape its flat side in an upward motion on the harbour wall. It is surprising just how productive this method can be at times. But the right conditions are vital – a quiet harbour, plenty of weed growth, and lots of stealth on the part of the netsman.

There is one invaluable tip which I must not forget to pass on regarding keeping shrimps, prawns etc alive in well oxygenated water whilst catching them. Procure a large plastic bucket or one of those polythene tubs with wire handles in which emulsion paint, putty and other decorator's supplies arrive. Mark it halfway up with a pencil line all round the outer circumference. Then, with a hot skewer or a 6in nail, puncture holes all around the upper half of the container. Whilst the live bait is being caught the bucket can be left standing in the sea water; when lifted out the top half will drain itself and in so doing oxygenate the bottom half. In a boat while bait is being caught, the bucket can be hung over the side with the rim well clear of the water so that the wave movement gently changes the water all the time. On a shoreline, instead of the water having to be tipped out and changed, with the risk of losing the bait, the 'colander' type bucket is merely dipped into a pool and lifted in and out once or twice to change the water effectively. At all times the bottom half still retains enough water depth to keep the bait alive and fresh.

When wading around in rocky pools netting out prawns and push-netting for shrimps in shallow water on the beach, quite a number of small, live rock-pool fish can be caught and retained for use later as both live and dead baits. The butterfish (or gunnel) and the various types of blennies, together with small eels (both conger and freshwater), are all excellent baits which can easily be kept alive for long periods.

At this point, I am certain that a few of my readers will question the use, on ethical grounds, of live creatures for bait. Such matters are eternally controversial and I will merely say that each angler should decide for himself where his feelings lie and then let his conscience dictate to him how he is going to carry out his fishing. But above all, if he is an anti-livebaiter, I would respectfully suggest that he does not adopt a holier-than-thou attitude to the angler who impales a small live fish on a hook in order to attract something large and voracious.

One of the great mysteries of sea angling (a conundrum I have personally grappled with for years) is the hardback and 'peeler crab' puzzle. Only one species of sea fish is regularly taken on hardback crab hook offerings, and that is the wrasse. Yet I have on many occasions, while gutting cod fresh from the sea, emptied out their stomach contents and found, among the various small dead fish and marine worms, large live shore crabs which I have released, to see them scuttle hurriedly away. This is one of the eternal riddles of sea angling. Softbacked crabs are a deadly bait for a great many species, whilst hardbacked crabs can be dismissed as an ineffective bait except for those toothy crab and shellfish crunchers: the bottom-grubbing wrasse.

All this angling jargon about 'softbacks', 'hardbacks' and 'peelers' will be baffling to anyone who is not familiar with the life cycle of crabs. To put it simply, the crab continuously outgrows its shell and at various times, usually between May and September, rejects the old one and hides itself away for a week or so until the new one underneath hardens up. To name just two fish which are avid eaters of 'soft' and 'peeler' crabs, I will mention bass and cod in particular, but many other species find crab baits irresistible. Unfortunately the great snag with this bait is that it is not generally available as a tackle shop supply. Rocky, weedy, muddy shorelines are the favourite habitat of crabs, and good 'peeler' collecting ground is usually well worked over by the few professional crab gatherers and also a host of angling collectors as well.

At this point, I will clear up a bothersome question of the legality of crab collecting. The common shore crab, which is greenish-brown, is not protected by law and can be taken in all sizes. However, the edible crab, which is pinkish-brown, is protected by fishery laws and must not be taken except above the normal eating size. The exact measurements are apt to vary from one part of the coastline to another. I am aware that these regulations are contravened by a great many anglers, and some writers as well, who with tongue in cheek shamelessly recommend the female edible crab as a killing bass bait when it is at the 'peeler' or 'softback' stage and is of a size comparable with a 50p piece across the back section. Nevertheless, I feel obliged to quote the law as it stands and leave anglers to comply with it as their conscience dictates. One thing is certain. If we blatantly flout the Fishery Laws ourselves, we cannot with any justification complain about trawler crews and commercial fishing operators doing likewise so far as other aspects of fish and marine life conservation are concerned.

Summertime is the crab collector's heyday and on a good

weedy, rocky estuarial shoreline, where the tide just creeps in and out again without any violent wave action, the conditions for crabbing will be ideal. Two punctured bait buckets will serve as crab holders and the crab operator should be equipped with thick thigh waders to keep his knees dry when he kneels down. A stout pair of gardening gloves will protect his hands from the sharp barnacle-covered rocks – and the odd weever fish – and a strong wire or mild steel crab-hook, to lift up the seaweed curtains and poke around into the holes in the rocks, is the correct tool for crabbing.

Moulting crabs fully realise what a vulnerable state they are in and accordingly their instincts tell them to hide away until their shells harden up again. In the 'peeler' or 'softback' state they are very docile and do not rear up with outstretched claws to defend themselves like 'hardbacks' do. Whenever you find two crabs mounted 'in tandem' with a very angry cock crab uppermost, you can be quite certain that the crab below is a female in moult. Separate them and place the female in one of your bait containers. Incidentally the reason for having two separate bait buckets is so that the 'softbacks' can be kept segregated from the 'peelers'. Obviously the softbacks, which have already shed their shells and are in the process of hardening up, need using first. The peelers, however, can be kept for a considerable period before they shed their shells and are then ready to be used as hookbait.

To recognise 'softbacks' and 'peelers' at a glance takes quite some practice and a few years of shoreline experience. Here, for the raw beginner, I will list some of the pointers and tests which can be made to ascertain which is which when crab hunting. 'Softbacks' are easily recognised if their backs are gently pressed with a thumb nail; the shell will be found to be soft and quite yielding if the crab has just rid itself of its old shell. After a day or two this new shell will begin to harden, but if the crab is in a reasonably 'soft' state it will still make a very good hookbait if used immediately it is collected.

'Peelers' are harder to figure out. On some of them the shell will just be lifting at the rear of the crab, but on others it will still be in place and the angler will be faced with a border line decision. Is it, or is it not, a potential 'peeler?' The final test in such a case is to take one of the crab's rear legs in your hand and with finger and thumb gently pull it near the tip. If the crab is almost ready to peel, this leg portion will come away in your fingers leaving the new shell covering underneath: rather like an outer skin being removed. Conversely, if the leg tip portion resists removal and feels quite firm and strongly attached, leave well alone and release the crab. It is a hardback and will not make a good bait in its present condition.

With great ingenuity quite a number of astute sea anglers are 'farming' peeler crabs in remote locations, so that they can be assured of a regular supply of crab bait throughout the summer 'peeler' months. As moulting crabs like to hide away in all manner of secure nooks and crannies, old curved roof tiles and short ends of agricultural clay drain pipes are partially buried in the mud and sand at selected locations so that the crabs will find a readymade haven of rest during their moult. To make this crab farming a worthwhile proposition, the location of the crab shelters should be kept a closely guarded secret and they must be in an area of shoreline where the casual exploring bait diggers will not chance to pass and observe what is going on. Otherwise, when the crab farmer visits his shoreline preserve to collect many delectable baits, he may find, to his extreme dismay, that a claim-jumper has preceded him and cleared out his crab colony.

'Peelers' and 'softbacks' can be stored for a few days in suitable containers if covered with wet seaweed and kept in a cool, dark place away from direct sunlight. For lengthy storage, aerated water and the controlled temperature conditions of a marine aquarium set-up are necessary.

There is one other very good hook offering which will take bass, cod, all the members of the flatfish species and thornback rays. I am referring to that very interesting sea creature, the hermit crab, of course. It can be caught by 'dropnetting' from off harbour and breakwater walls. Like the whelk it is rather difficult to remove from its living accommodation. To call it its 'shell' would be quite wrong as the hermit crab does not have a shell of its own; it very ingeniously occupies an empty shell found on the sea bed and its choice of home is usually a vacant whelk shell.

Hermit crabs can either be used whole or with the 'crab head' part nipped off so that the soft, lower body portion is placed on the hook. To extract them from the shell is rather difficult. Perhaps the best method is to crack open, with a small hammer, the sharp end of the shell wherein the crab's tail is housed with hooks which provide it with a firm grip. Once this tail has been exposed, the whole hermit crab can be gently eased out of the protective shell.

Squid is a very long lasting (if deep frozen) convenience bait, which is tough so that it stays on the hook and withstands hard casting. Bass and cod love it, especially if it is used as the main hook offering and tipped with marine worm bait, rag or lugworm, to make a large, juicy cocktail bait.

Before the arrival of the many foreign visitors we now have dwelling with us, there was no demand for squid as a food for humans and literally tons of it were thrown back overboard by trawler crews. Today the situation has undergone a rapid change and we are actually importing foreign squid in freezer pack boxes to supplement the supplies we catch ourselves. With a box of frozen squid at the bottom of his freezer (which the dear wife cannot possibly object to as it can be classed as a 'food item'), the enthusiastic shore fisherman can be assured of a good supply of bait always on tap. Provided of course that he can remember to remove what he needs at least twelve hours before his fishing trip so that it has ample time to thaw out.

The last group of baits in this chapter are the oily fishes: mackerel, herrings, pilchards and sprats. If taken fresh from the sea and deep frozen, they are, like squid, a marvellously handy convenience bait. But their use, I find, is strictly regional and they are on a par with mussel in being used only in certain geographical areas. For instance, on the Yorkshire coast, and further north as well, shorecasters seem to have very little faith in fish baits. They put their trust in the universal lugworm, mussel and to a lesser extent crab hook offerings, completely scorning the oily fish baits which are extensively used by shore anglers on the South coast.

As a shorefishing bait for conger, when casting is being done from rocks which give on to deep water, there is nothing to surpass a fresh mackerel head which has been severed neatly from the body, with the guts still attached and trailing in an attractively scent-wafting manner. To present half fish portions, side fillets and strips of fish bait properly, a very keen, thin-bladed filleting knife and a cutting board are necessary so that the job can be carried out with finesse. Get your victim on the operating table, take up your razor-sharp knife and make a really neat job of the bait cutting 'operation'.

In recent years, as the popularity of mullet fishing has spread, a great many coarse fishing baits have been adopted by sea anglers. Bread in the form of 'flake', paste and crust has proved deadly once the fish have been educated to take it by the liberal use of a free offering of groundbait made up from stale well dampened mashed loaves. On a number of occasions I have sat myself down on a tidal river with traditional coarse fishing tackle and maggots for bait and taken a mixed bag of mullet, dabs and flounders, all of which accepted such an unusual hook offering with apparent relish.

8
Natural Elements Which Affect Shorefishing

The shore angler does not usually take such a weighty catch of fish as his counterpart who fishes in really deep water from a boat, nor is he liable to land such a variety of species. But one great point in the shorecaster's favour is that he is very rarely prevented from fishing by adverse weather conditions. If a force 8 gale is blowing, the beach man can usually find a sheltered estuary or harbour with fairly calm water. Not so the angling mariner. With gloomy face, he listens to the radio weather forecast or alternatively rings up his local coastguard station and then, in the interests of safety, motors home to put his bait back into the deep freezer. At odd times, often right in the middle of the busy holiday season, when the weather has been particularly diabolical, the charter angling fleets, located mainly on the South coast, have been what is known as 'blown off' and remained tied up in port for weeks on end. Quite a trying time financially, if your living is dependent upon the vagaries of our highly unreliable English weather.

On open shorelines, if the tides dictate where you can fish and at what time of day, the strength and direction of the wind most certainly has the final word in governing 'if you can fish'. But happily, unlike the poor old boat fishermen, shore anglers can adopt a different attitude to bad weather forecasts without putting themselves into any danger. If gales are imminent, but the sea is not yet rough enough to make fishing impossible, then the shore angler can be down on the tide line enjoying his sport – provided that he is not foolish enough to occupy a fishing position on an exposed headland where a sudden gust of wind may rear up a freak wave that would wash him off. Similarly, immediately a gale is beginning to abate a little, and as soon as the subsidence of the waves makes fishing possible, the shorecaster can be in action again with his tackle, as long as he is sensible in his choice of fishing venue and does not take unnecessary risks in tricky situations.

In order to acquire a thorough knowledge of the local tidal movements, the aspiring shore fisherman should first of all equip himself with two vital items, and these should be studied diligently before he even thinks of buying a rod. Number one is the shorefisher's Bible, which goes under the common name of a tide table. The second thing, which is almost as important, is a calendar with the moon phases clearly shown. The new moon and full moon phase indications, which on my calendar are shown as bold red squares with a white crescent moon and a large round full moon, are of vital importance. The highest and most powerful spring (nothing to do with the seasons – just tidal terminology) tides occur at these times. Hang this calendar in a place where you can continually glance at it; by doing so you will soon become absolutely familiar with the tidal patterns.

Your gospel according to the tide table will tell you that there are two tides per day. The 'height of water' column will also give you a clear indication in feet (and metres) of the rise and fall of the water level. This varies around the coast tremendously; for instance, the Bristol Channel and the Channel Islands have a rise of approximately 45ft, whereas on the West coast of Ireland the big spring tides only give a total rise of about 6ft. To complicate matters further, although it is generally accepted that there are two tides per day, some areas of coastline have what are known as 'double tides'. In the Solent area a most unusual tidal flow occurs. Initially the flood tide moves in a westerly direction; then a second conflicting high tide occurs when the ebb from the direction of France conflicts with the ebbing of the first high tide.

To clarify the situation of tidal flows and to get a clear mental picture in your mind's eye of what happens so far as 'springs' and 'neaps' are concerned, try to memorise the following basic rules.

106

...gging deep boring
...worms with a
...fter' (rabbiting,
...ining or trenching
...de). For single
...ded lugworm
...ging, on certain
...ts of the coast, this
...he only tool which
... enable the angler
...dig deep enough at
...ed to extract the
...eating worm

...ditional long
...dled three-tined
...dworm fork. The
...l digging tool for
...dy beaches

A good crabbing shoreline should have plenty of large boulders with seaweed curtains hanging around them. An old blunt gaff and a wire 'crab hook' will make the operation easier

A simple home-made push net will provide the shorecaster with a host of bait items from the inshore shallows

Tides are caused by the force of gravity exerted upon the earth's water masses by both the sun and the moon. Spring tides happen fortnightly: at new moon, when the moon is in a position exactly between the sun and the earth, and at full moon, when the earth is in a position between the sun and the moon. On these occasions, the pull of gravity on the earth, by the moon and the sun, is in a straight line, which means that a great force is exerted upon the earth and its water. Conversely, the neap tides happen also every fortnight when the moon is in the first quarter and the third quarter. At these times the moon and the sun are at 90 degree angles to the earth. Therefore their gravitational forces are in opposition to each other and a lesser force is exerted upon the earth's water masses.

Very simply explained in non-technical language which I will call 'Forsberg-isms', the spring tides can be called 'bigs' and the neap tides 'littles'. The 'bigs' take place at new and full moon and last a week, building up in water height gradually three days before, peaking at the day of the moon phase, and dropping off for three days afterwards to give a complete cycle of seven days. Likewise, the 'neaps' or 'littles' take place in the intervals between the 'bigs' and they also last a week. So in a lunar month of approximately 29 days we have: a 'big' and a 'little', a 'big' and a 'little', all one week each which neatly fills in the month. A glance at your moon phase calendar will make it all crystal clear.

One great mystery which confirmed landlubbers find hard to grasp is the fact that, although the tides advance and retreat up and down the shoreline, the actual tidal flow is a lateral movement along the shore rather than an in-and-out one. Anyone casting a leaded terminal tackle into a strong flooding or ebbing tide will soon be convinced of this aspect of tidal movement. If a very light bomb-type sinker is used without grapnel wires, the strong water flow will roll it along the beach and it will eventually end up quite near to the water's edge with the line running almost parallel to the beach.

The times of the tides advance approximately forty minutes each day, so that a 12 noon Monday high tide this week will have shifted itself forward to a tea time 5 o'clock tide on the same day next week. Likewise, this week's Monday midnight tide will have advanced to a 5 am tide next week on the same day. Neap tides do not come very far up the beach, neither do they retreat very far back down again. Also, as they do not have a great volume of water to move, their flow is quite gentle. Conversely, big spring tides are most powerful since they must in their twelve-hour cycle advance very far up the shoreline and also retreat a long way back down again. A slack water period of varying duration occurs at dead high and dead low water as the tide changes over from ebb to flow, or flow to ebb.

A careful study of the tides, local currents and the geographical peculiarities of the surrounding shoreline is of inestimable value to the sea angler when he must try to decide where and when to fish or dig his bait. Wind direction is of critical importance when an open sea beach is the proposed fishing venue. Offshore winds, if they are strong, flatten off the waves and often produce a calming influence for a distance of perhaps half a mile out to sea, especially if the shoreline is bounded by steep cliffs which afford a sheltering effect. This is even more pronounced if the water is almost up to them and the angler is fishing on a narrow strip of beach between the tide line and the cliff bottom. In such circumstances, I have fished with a raging force 9 gale whistling high up overhead; but down below all was calm and peaceful, with the sea surface like a millpond, for perhaps a mile from the shore, until it suddenly became rough where the full force of the wind caught it away from the shelter of the cliffs.

Onshore and oblique side winds are a different matter. These can be of great benefit to the angler or spoil his sport altogether. A moderate onshore blow, which is not too strong, can produce a short choppy sea which will so oxygenate the water that the fish are right close in among the breakers and feeding avidly. On a very gently shelving shoreline such a wind will invariably produce a wonderful series of flat foaming water tables which stretch for a great distance from the shore. These are ideal deep water wading bass conditions, especially if an onshore gale has been forecast and the wind is beginning to strengthen and the sea roughen up a little after a long period of flat calm.

A gale force onshore wind which brings huge pounding breakers and flying spume is the absolute kiss of death to all angling activities on open beaches and exposed rock marks. In such conditions the fish have sensibly swum out into deeper water to escape the churned up sand and silt and the turmoil down below. To attempt to fish in such stormy seas is foolish. The surf will run a great distance up the beach and the water will be absolutely thick with great strands of weed and, on some parts of the coast, huge mats of uprooted kelp stalks.

A great problem faced by all shore anglers is that of determining just how rough the sea has to be before fishing is impossible. The ability to judge accurately if your terminal tackle will just hold bottom or alternatively be swept along the shoreline is a kind of sixth sense development which is only acquired after long fishing experience. To view a breaking sea from a high cliff is no good whatsoever; from such a raised vantage point the waves look far smaller than they actually are. The most reliable way to appraise the roughness of the sea and the size of the breakers is to get right down at beach level and look at them from a fishing position.

For those anglers who have a long distance to travel before they reach the coast, the rough sea aspect can be infuriating. General weather forecasts and coastguard station reports, whilst being quite helpful, in no way give a direct indication to the shore angler whether he can fish or not on his arrival. The only foolproof way I know of getting on-the-spot appraisals of the shorefishing conditions is to arrange with an angler who lives at the prospective venue to view the shoreline just before you are due to set off and give his candid opinion of the weather over the telephone. This is a wise course of action which will save endless expense and frustration.

9
The Art of Safe, Trouble-free Casting

A great deal of shameless, misleading bunkum is constantly being bandied about on the sea angling scene, with regard to long distance casting. A couple of decades ago, the aim of every aspiring beachcaster was to attain the magical distance of 100 yards, or a 'ton-up' cast as it later became known. Then, with the lightning speed-up in the development of rod and reel design, the 100yd cast was rapidly left behind and the distance began to creep ever upwards towards the 200yd mark. Here, I must hasten to add an explanation which will clarify the whole situation of distance casting. As in other outdoor sports, the makers of the equipment are constantly scrambling to outdo each other in the performance of their products and thereby grab the lion's share of the retail market. To this end, tackle manufacturers take on to their design staff expert casters who invariably make their name on the tournament casting scene, which to my way of viewing is a sport more aligned to athletics than actual fish catching.

So we have a peculiar situation where highly trained athletes make truly prodigious casts (and equally embarrassing crack-offs) – now exceeding a distance of 250yd – on special grass courts under absolutely ideal conditions, and their feats are published alongside rod and reel performance advertisements. All of which is very misleading to the beachcasting beginner who is led to believe that, if he buys one of the special 'named' rods, he can go down to the shoreline and do likewise. Very sad when our raw angling recruit, after purchasing an identical set of the gear which, to quote the tackle 'blurb', 'broke the 200yd casting barrier', finds to his dismay that, with a trailing hook link and a big bait, on a shoreline where his footing is insecure and there is a strong side wind blowing, his casts barely reach the 70 or 80yd mark.

To put the whole business of distance casting into the right perspective, let me here and now give some sensible comparisons between grass court casting and actual, on the shoreline, fishing. First and most important, the fish do not start at 100 yards out; fish are usually where the food is and if that place is 50 yards offshore, the long distance exponent will be over-casting them. As a rough guide, I would say that it is sensible to halve a casting court distance when thinking in terms of using the same tackle on the beach with bait added and slippery rocks underfoot.

Let no one be misled by the foregoing statements. The ability to cast long distances with great accuracy is of paramount importance at certain times, either when the fish are well offshore or when a certain small area of the shoreline is a hotspot that is producing all the fish. However, long, smooth, trouble-free casting ability cannot be bought over the counter of a tackle shop with a big wad of pound notes. The rod and the reel, no matter how expensive or well designed, cannot, by their perfection, compensate for the faulty, jerky casting style of the person who is using them and totally obviate the errors he makes while performing his casting movements.

One great psychological hang-up which most aspiring beach-casters suffer is the truly traumatic experience of making their first appearance on the shoreline with a brand-new set of tackle and providing unlimited entertainment for the 'old hands' who stand around and laugh heartily when things go wrong. There are two obvious ways to counteract such an embarrassing situation. If your impatience to catch a fish will not let you go on to a secluded sports field for a practice session, then do the next best thing, and make your mistakes unseen and unlaughed at on some remote shoreline where you are all alone with your ragged technique.

So far as casting instruction is concerned, I have great

reservations about recommending such a course of action to the amateur. If you can find someone who is a really competent instructor, then your troubles are almost over, because he will rapidly assess what you are doing wrong and rectify your mistakes. But be eternally wary of self-styled experts. Like car driving, correct casting should be taught in a proper manner by someone with a sound technique and the ability to teach, recognise initial imperfections, and eradicate bad habits. Otherwise all the pupil will do is emulate the style and faults of his instructor.

Before the first casts are made, there are certain preparations to the tackle which can be carried out to smooth the path of the caster and cut down 'crack-offs', and over-runs if a multiplier reel is being used. First and foremost, new nylon monofilament line is apt to be rather stiff and prone to throwing off the reel in coils, especially if a fixed-spool reel is being used. To 'mature' the line a little, so that it beds down snugly on the reel and comes off easily during a cast, run it all out, with a lead weight on the end, preferably over damp grass. Then reel it in steadily, ensuring that it is wound on to the reel in neatly ordered layers with no loose coils or 'humps' on the reel spool. Carry out this operation at least four or five times to break the line in a little and make sure it has lost the tendency to spring up in coils off the reel, or twist itself into loops.

So far as fixed-spool reels are concerned, they require very little pre-casting preparation apart from a brief check to see that they are well oiled and working properly, with the correct loading of line which comes up to within one eighth of an inch of the lip of the spool. Multiplier reels, however, are a totally different proposition; they require tuning to the individual casting style of the person who is going to use them. There are different methods of doing this. Expensive reels which incorporate built-in mechanical and centrifugal adjustable braking systems are the simplest to deal with. For a start, to find out how the reel will perform when casting is being done, put a pair of the largest brake blocks in the centrifugal braking system (there are three sizes, small, medium and large) and adjust the mechanical one so that the reel spool revolves quite freely when the casting weight is hung on to the line and the free spool mechanism is engaged. Although these adjustments will usually give a rather sluggish reel performance, they will at least ensure that catastrophic over-runs are not met with during those rather jerky casting movements which every beginner makes when he first attempts to operate his tackle.

On the cheaper variety of multiplier reels, which have no automatic braking system whatsoever, this business of reel 'tuning' is a little more complicated. To slow down the spool, different grades of motor car engine oil can be used in the bearings or on the spindle housings. This will produce a very sluggish movement when the reel is put into 'free spool' and have almost the same effect as the braking systems, if the oiling is done successfully.

Correct line loading on the spools of multiplier reels is vital for good casting performance. If your casting ability is such that only 150 yards, or less, of line are in use, what is the point in loading up a large, wide drummed reel with 300 yards of line? The added weight of line on the spool produces excessive inertia which makes correct thumb control exceedingly difficult, with the result that over-runs occur. Far better to buy a narrow drummed reel which holds less line and delivers it up through the rod rings in better alignment than to use a broad drummed reel where the line zig-zags from side to side as it is thrown off the reel spool during casting.

At this point we come up against the most controversial aspect of the whole affair: namely the personal safety factor of casting. Put quite bluntly, your 5 or 6oz lead in full flight at the beginning of a powerful cast is a potential killer if either of two things happen. One: some unfortunate person is standing quite near the caster and is struck on the head as the lead arcs round in the power stroke. Two, and even more horrific: the lead 'cracks-off' due to a line breakage, and goes flying away perhaps at head level down a crowded shoreline or along a pier where lots of

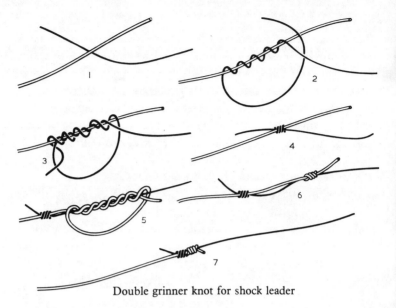

Double grinner knot for shock leader

unsuspecting holidaymakers are strolling. Two different kinds of safety precautions can be taken by the beachcasting exponent. The one which is most widely used is known as the 'shock leader' or 'casting piece'. The other (a cause of endless arguments) is the limiting of casting styles so that those which are known to be potentially dangerous are not carried out except when there is absolutely no risk to bystanders, other anglers or distant shore walkers.

The 'casting piece' or 'shock leader' will obviate most of the line breakages which would otherwise take place when very powerful casts are being made with main reel lines below the 20lb breaking strain mark and leads between 4 and 8oz. The extra strong casting leader, which should be at least 30ft long to give sufficient length so that it runs up from the lead in the casting position, down the full length of the rod, and allows at least six turns on the spool of the reel, is knotted securely to the reel line by means of a double grinner knot – a joining method which I have found utterly reliable. As a rough guide, a 4oz lead requires a 35 to 40lb breaking strain leader, 5oz 40 to 50lb and 6 to 8oz 45 to 55lb.

Personally, I do not like using shock leaders for beach fishing. They have three inherent drawbacks. Right at the start of the cast, the leader knot is liable to slash a deep gash in the casting reel thumb if it is not located at the side of the reel spool before the cast is made. In addition, the noise from the knot is rather unnerving, as it flies upwards through the rod rings with a series of jerks. Also, from a tackle operating point of view, if there is a lot of loose weed floating around in the water, on reeling in the shock leader knot gathers up a great bunch of it which prevents the line being reeled in past the tip ring, where the weed jams up in a solid mass – an infuriating happening if you are playing the fish of a lifetime. Finally, if you get snagged up with a strong leader on and pull for a break, it invariably happens that your weaker reel line snaps just near your reel, or at the rod end, and a great deal of line is lost, including all the terminal tackle. This catastrophe is averted if you use a level reel line without a leader and a 'reduced breaking strain' terminal rig set-up.

So far as casting styles are concerned, I view the current craze for distance at all costs as extremely irresponsible and dangerous. The basic, safe, beginners' cast, popularly known as the 'layback' (which I shall describe in detail shortly) is one where the rod tip travels in a more or less straightforward movement from shore to sea. If this cast is executed smoothly, in a perfectly controlled manner, there is very little danger from 'crack-offs', and a casting leader is not necessary if a 'straight through' main reel line of about 25–30lb breaking strain is used with a 5 or 6oz lead and a slow or medium taper rod.

Exaggerated casting styles, where great powerful side-swipe arcs of the rod tip are made to build up rod compression and tip velocity, with the amount of 'dangle' from rod tip to lead being almost as long as the rod, and with the lead swinging to and fro pendulum style or even laid out on the ground behind the caster, are techniques which certainly produce great distances. But the safety factor in such tournament casting styles is sadly lacking. Some angling clubs ban what is known as the 'pendulum' and 'South African' cast altogether in the interests of ensuring that

117

Layback cast

their members stay alive and enjoy their fishing. It is not for me to sit in judgement on such matters, but merely to point the way to safety in casting and leave the angler to work out his own salvation so far as regard for other beach users is concerned. Whatever kind of casting you finally aspire to and become proficient at, always bear in mind the fact that the caster is at the centre of the activity and rarely gets clobbered by his own lead. Those in the 'spin-off' area are most liable to get hit by beachcasting 'fall-out', and if your rod arc is somewhere in the 270 degree range, the 'safe' area is very small indeed.

In recommending the layback cast as the right one for a beginner to start on, I have the other beach users' safety uppermost in my mind. I am also convinced that the simplicity of it will instantly appeal to the amateur caster, as there are no violent body gyrations involved and no intricate foot-shift movements either. Also, this cast can comfortably be performed on an uneven shoreline composed of large boulders, or even on slippery green weed, provided that the angler is wearing suitably studded boots which give his feet the firmest grip possible.

To commence the layback cast with the normal beachcasting gear, which will be 12ft rod, multiplier reel, 25–30lb monofilament line, and a 5 or 6oz lead with a single hook paternoster terminal tackle, the caster, presuming he is right-handed, will take up a position sideways on to the sea with feet comfortably apart about shoulder width. Left foot and left shoulder will be nearest to the sea, which is the direction that the cast will take when the lead is released. The rod is held across the body, with the left hand on the rod butt, and the right hand positioned just below the multiplier reel so that the right thumb falls comfortably onto the reel spool.

With the weight of the body firmly on the back, right foot, the rod is extended away from the sea with about three or four feet of terminal tackle, ending in the lead, hanging from the rod tip. The reel is in the downward position with the spool towards the ground so that the rod rings face downwards and the caster can then glance along the rod to make sure all the line is running free through the rod rings with no sign of a loop around the tip ring. At this point, when the caster is ready to go into his forward drive and commence the cast, two vitally important things must happen. First, he should make sure that the multiplier reel is in 'free spool', by flicking over the appropriate lever with his left hand. The right hand, of course, is kept near the reel so that the thumb controls the spool and prevents it revolving when the left hand releases the free-spool lever.

Second, I will come out with a time-honoured tip of mine which is called the 'drop-down' technique. It is especially useful when fishing in the dark. You need to be absolutely positive before you commence the cast that the reel is really in 'free-spool' and the line is running free through the rings with no unnoticed twists or loops round the tip ring. After the 'free-spool' lever has been activated, the right thumb is just eased up off the reel spool a fraction so that the spool can revolve for a turn or two which will allow the lead weight dangling from the rod tip to pull down a foot or so of line. This wise precaution just before the start of the cast acts as a safety check to make sure that the 'free-spool' lever has been operated. Also of paramount importance, it ensures that the line is all running free through the rings from reel spool to rod tip, a most important aspect when you are fishing in the dark and cannot make a visual check of the rod end. With all systems switched to 'Go' and the reel in free spool with the line running unhampered through the rod rings, the caster is poised to begin the forward power drive which will produce enough compression in the rod to propel the terminal tackle forward way out to sea in a long, smooth curving trajectory.

The cardinal rule of good casting is to let the rod do all the work and make all the body movements smooth and perfectly co-ordinated; there is no room for brute force in perfect casting. To that end, the caster now begins the forward rod movement, aiming to sweep the rod smoothly approximately over his right shoulder with the right hand pushing strongly and the left hand guiding the butt section to complete a well controlled, smooth turn-over of the rod. At the start of the cast, the whole of the body weight was on the back right foot. As the rod is swept overhead, the weight of the body is smoothly transferred to the left foot (the one nearest to the sea) so that a perfectly balanced follow-through of the rod can be made.

I am sure that the hardest part of this cast is knowing exactly when to lift the reel thumb which is securely locking the spool, so that the lead is released at precisely the right moment when the rod begins its forward power drive. If you hold on too long, instead of flying forward and away, the sinker will arc down and splash into the sea only a short distance away. Conversely, by releasing the thumb too soon, the lead will fly upwards high into the air as the rod is still being 'turned-over', and splash down only a short way out.

Getting the sixth sense intuition which allows the caster to release his lead at exactly the right time only comes with constant practice. I find that the easiest way to overcome this problem of lead release is to slow everything right down and just perform very gentle initial casts while you are unsure of yourself and still learning to cast. Speed and power will come later as you attain perfect reel control and co-ordination. By making gentle, short casts at first, you will obtain perfect reel control and obviate serious over-runs which produce enormous tangling of line on the reel spool.

As your first casts are liable to be far too 'beefy' and powerful, it is advisable to wear some form of thumb protector: a finger stall, the thumb piece cut from an old rubber glove, or even a thick strip of sticking plaster. To develop what is called an 'educated thumb' takes many years of casting practice with a multiplier reel. There are two schools of thought on where exactly you should thumb the reel. One set of theorists maintain that the shoulder of the spool should be braked with thumb pressure and the thumb should at all times be clear of the actual reel line. On the other hand, I and many others feel that the thumb should be on the line in the middle of the spool. This gives perfect 'feel' of the line as the spool is revolving. At the slightest sign of a 'line lift' or 'rattle', which is the forerunner of an over-run, the spool can be instantly slowed down by the hovering thumb and a 'crack-off' or a 'tangle' prevented.

On the tackle market at the present time there are a number of attachable mechanical braking devices for multiplier reels. They are all aimed at either cutting down over-runs and back-lashes or giving the reel thumb some mechanical braking assistance. Doubtless many more ingenious appliances will appear to smooth the rather thorny path of the multiplier user. Without hesitation I am always willing to doff my fishing hat (battered and muddy though it may be) to the nimble-brained originators of such cunning devices. I suffered many burned thumbs and cracked-off terminal tackles as a multiplier apprentice, and my finances were always stretched as I paid out every fishing trip for hundreds of yards of badly snarled line which I had to carve off the reel spool.

So far as the side-cast and the fixed-spool reels are concerned, casting with them, in comparison to a multiplier, is child's play; hence their enormous popularity. The lay-back cast is quite suitable for both side-cast and fixed-spool tackle set-ups. By using

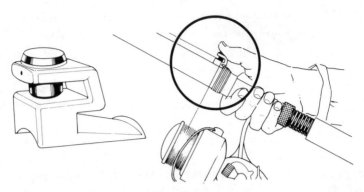

Thumb button

a 'thumb button' whipped to the rod when casting with the fixed-spool reel, the bogey of sliced index fingers will be entirely obviated. Failing a 'thumb button', a thick protective glove on the reel hand, or even a good wrapping of surgical tape on the reel release 'index' finger, will prevent cuts through casting accidents and line slip.

The critical test of any casting technique comes when the angler attempts to perform in the dark. In pitch blackness he really must use the 'drop-down' 'free line' method to ensure that his tackle is all running free. In order to make the 'drop-down' check easier, I always incorporate a quick release line swivel attachment in my terminal tackle between the reel line and the sinker so that there is exactly three feet of line between the swivel and the lead. In the dark, I merely wind up the lead towards the rod tip until I feel the swivel check at the top ring. Then when I have engaged 'free-spool' on the reel, it is a simple matter to lift my thumb slightly to let a further six inches or a foot of line slip through the rod rings to tell me that I am running free on all systems.

Lots of beginners have a great fear of casting in the dark with a multiplier reel because they cannot follow the flight of the lead with their eyes and check the reel spool with the thumb the moment the lead splashes down into the sea. The only way I know to overcome this drawback is to concentrate during daylight on the reel spool. Watch the line flowing off it and get the feel of it with your reel thumb. Once you get used to controlling the cast with the thumb and are able to cast smoothly without always watching the lead, you will build up sufficient daylight casting confidence to do the same automatically in the dark.

As a parting shot, I will briefly explain the mechanics of the 'Scarborough tackle' cast. This is for the sole benefit of those few adventurous souls who, at some future date in their chequered fishing careers, may fancy operating from a high rock platform or precipitous cliff mark with this stiff pole and 'cartwheel' minority group category of rock and kelp mark fishing gear. At the outset, I must explain that the Scarborough-type rod 'heaves' the tackle out seawards rather than casts it. This is due to the fact that the reel is large in circumference and hard to 'get started' revolving, and the rod is very stiff and unbending and designed for pulley-hauling rather than casting and playing in fish with the usual beachcasting rod flexibility. One peculiarity about the way the Scarborough reel is made to function is that it is 'backwound' in an anti-clockwise direction when line is recovered. The reason for this unorthodox method of reeling in is so that when a cast is made the line flows off the top of the reel through the rings in a very smooth direct line, rather than at an acute angle from the bottom of the reel drum, which is of course exceptionally large when compared with other sea fishing centre-pin reels.

The traditional stance for Scarborough casting is with your back to the sea at the commencement of the cast, and this unnerves most beginners, especially if they are perched on a narrow rock ledge with a 200ft drop beneath them! Quite a long length of terminal tackle 'drop' is used for Scarborough casting, and to trap the line securely whilst the powerful side-swipe swing is being made the fingers of the uppermost hand curl round the rod a few feet above the low positioned reel and the line is gripped by the index finger, trapping it securely against the rod. The reel hand has a very important function to carry out. The first and second fingers of the reel hand, which incidentally is positioned just below the reel, act as a delicate braking mechanism at the end of the cast. They also hover just on the rim of the reel throughout the cast to slow it down a little should an over-run be in the offing. Before any attempt is made at executing the Scarborough cast with the appropriate tackle for which it was intended to be used, it is a wise precaution to seek out someone who is proficient at it and watch him carefully for a couple of hours. This will imprint firmly on your mind's eye the exact sequence of casting motions which take place.

Having had an action replay demonstrated for your especial benefit, take yourself off to a high harbour wall with your stout pole and cart wheel and practise Scarborough casting. The high stance is necessary at first, in order to permit the caster to make gentle swings in his initial casting stages to master reel control with the lead dropping downwards. Once proficient, the shoulders can then be thrown back and the muscles flexed, and away goes the lead in a smooth powerful cast! Finally, bear in mind that a 'backlash' with a Scarborough outfit, if you are standing on a narrow ledge with your back to the sea, can be very dangerous. The jerk as the reel jams up solid and the lead tries to continue horizonwards could sufficiently unbalance the caster to cause him to topple over the edge of the rocks and down into the sea. Therefore until you become a real high ledge expert, stand a little back from sheer drops as a self-preservation safety precaution.

The author in action on a deserted playing field at 5 am on a summer morning. This is the only safe place to practise those fancy 'tournament style' casts if you wish to steer clear of manslaughter charges

The ideal sea conditions for bass fishing – long, flat 'water tables' with foam in the shallow water

Sunday morning on Bournemouth Pier. For the gregarious sea angler this is an ideal location. (Note the drop-net to the left of the picture)

Casting for cod from Spurn Head peninsula, Humberside, in a winter sunset

10
Fish Which May Be Caught from Our Shoreline

I am quite certain that the average town dweller in this country, who lives perhaps a hundred miles from the sea and usually pays it a regular visit for his holidays every summer, has not the slightest conception of the truly amazing number of different fish species which inhabit the seas around this island. Most of them are residents, which may move around quite a lot, sometimes in vast shoals, up and down the coastline, often close inshore and then out to the deeps again. However, we do have regular visits from many rare and unusual fish which are ocean wanderers, particularly when one of our exceptional tropical summers causes our coastal waters to heat up to unprecedented temperature levels.

Since the film *Jaws*, a great deal of interest has been aroused in the life-style and ocean wanderings of sharks. It may come as a rather unpleasant surprise to ardent sea bathers to learn that around our coast, especially during hot weather, there are quite a number of places where very large sharks patrol within three or four hundred yards of popular holiday beaches. Indeed, at Crackington Haven, just south of Bude Bay in Cornwall, porbeagle sharks around the 400lb mark have been taken on rod and line from boats operating within easy swimming distance of the shore. Another popular shark hunting hotspot is the Isle of Wight. I am always amused to see how the reporting of captured sharks is handled by the press. The angling newspapers give such catches large headlines, with pin-sharp photographs of the massive teeth-filled jaws and the proud captor grinning hugely. Not so the local papers, who rely on sea swimming holidaymakers for their livelihood; they choose not to mention such happenings – it is bad for business.

For the interest of sea fishermen, however, I can announce that six species of sharks can regularly be found in British waters: porbeagles, makos and blues, which constitute the majority of the catches made by boat anglers, and thresher, six-gill and hammerhead, which are not so common. I am quite certain that most shore anglers do not envisage themselves tangling with a shark while fishing from the shoreline. However, such feats are decidedly not fictional or indeed impossible. Some years ago a blue shark of 72lb seized on the bait of a cod angler fishing from the famous Chesil Beach near Weymouth and almost pulled him into the sea; luckily his friend grabbed him round the waist as he was sliding seawards across the shingle and together they landed this unusual catch.

Shark fishing from the shore was also successfully practised on the West coast of Ireland at Liscannor Bay in County Clare in the early 1960s. The quarry were porbeagle sharks and the captor took them in sizes up to 145lb, with larger ones about double that figure, and even above, being lost due to the extreme difficulty of operating extra long gaffs from slippery rocks giving on to deep water. Contrary to the popular belief among sea anglers in general, the visits of sharks are not confined to the Atlantic coast waters of southern England and Ireland. The coast of Scotland is visited by sharks which are frequently caught in commercial fishing nets. The Yorkshire coast also has a regular run of sharks, with porbeagles and even large makos chopping fish in half while boat anglers are in the act of reeling them in. Porbeagles are often found dead after becoming entangled in trammel nets which are set in quite shallow inshore waters. Further offshore, I have on quite a few occasions seen large fish, which were obviously very big mako sharks, clearing the water in prodigious leaps – a habit for which this species of shark is particularly noted when it is being played on the end of a line.

In view of the fact that the record mako was 500lb, taken by a lady angler in 1971, off the Eddystone reef, my sightings of large leaping fish off Flamborough Head are not as fantastic as they may seem. The mako shark is a genuine ocean roamer which inhabits the surface layers of the sea down to a level of 50 or 60 feet, feeding, in our waters, on mackerel and herring. Is it any wonder therefore that, during the hottest of our summer weather, I am constantly in fear that a shark somewhere around our coastline will take a sudden fancy to a pair of dangling succulent bather's legs? Regardless of how much propaganda we swallow about our inshore waters being absolutely safe for bathers, the World Shark Attack file lists three incidents around these coasts about which I have never ever seen anything published.

Apart from these six species of sharks several other rather unusual fish visit our inshore waters – usually during the summer months. The basking shark is one but it is perfectly harmless as it is a creature which feeds on plankton; it was at one time, just after World War II, fished for commercially off the West coast of Scotland and the Hebrides. Tuna fish also visit our waters, usually on the mackerel grounds off Cornwall and they also appear off the North Yorkshire coast, an area where they were regularly caught before the war on rod and line. Sunfish, those great, round, ungainly looking sea creatures, are often caught by boat anglers. Rays bream stray into our waters from the Mediterranean area; a few are often washed up half dead or dying on our beaches, when a sudden cold snap in the autumn catches them in shallow water and they perish from the cold before they can swim off to warmer climes again.

Proceeding downward in size, and approaching the species of fish which are more commonly associated with the catches made by sea anglers, there are a number of mini-sharks, of which the tope is the largest. Truly the tope can be called 'the shorefisher's shark', as it attains a size comparable with the smaller blue sharks – up to about 60 or 70lb – and in shallow water gives a memorable fight, usually consisting of a series of spool-whirring runs which can strip, in seconds, the whole of the line off a multiplier reel.

129

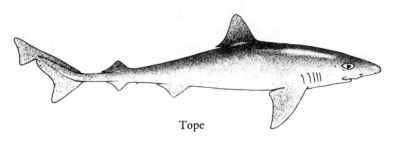

Tope

Tope are generally regarded as a summer species. They hunt their food over sandy bottoms where there is an abundance of flatfish, small members of the cod family, whiting, pouting and codling, and plenty of crabs and other small crustaceans, and their favourite feeding grounds seem to be in the mouths of broad shallow estuaries where there is a good, strong run of tide. For a great many years the distribution of tope was considered to be mainly in the southern half of England and all around the Irish coast. However, as sea angling has spread itself around a little so that the whole of Scotland has received some angling attention, a fresh picture has emerged. It is now known beyond doubt that tope can be caught around the whole of the British Isles in greater or lesser numbers, according to the suitability of the various locations. In shorefishing, anglers visiting remote virgin territory are apt to consider that they have discovered certain fish species which were not there before. What a truly erroneous assumption that can be. Usually the fish have been resident in such areas for a great many years; it is the anglers who were missing. It therefore pays to have a completely open mind on the subject of fish distribution; hard and fast rules do not apply to sea fish – like the tides, they are constantly on the move.

A further member of the mini-shark species which is often confused with the tope, because it is of a very similar appearance, is the smoothhound, of which there are two species. I shall not baffle my readers with their Latin names; suffice it to say that one has spots and the other has none. These fish come close inshore during the summer months, mainly around the south-eastern area of England. They feed on crabs, lobsters and prawns and

130

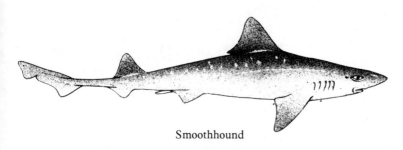
Smoothhound

chiefly move around in muddy, rocky, weedy estuarial waters and in shallow creeks where a great number of crabs abound.

To round off our appraisal of mini-sharks which the shore-fisher may tangle with, a brief mention of the dogfish family is necessary. Some anglers absolutely loathe the species and are apt to fly into a rage and stamp all over them if they chance to catch one. Other fishermen view them as a tasty meal, however, once the tough skin has been 'wrestled' off them and they have been chopped up into manageable chunks and deep fried in very hot fat. The most popular of the dogfish family is the greater spotted dogfish which can attain a weight in the region of 20lb. This fish is known as the bull huss and is greatly relished by fish and chip eaters in the London and South coast area. Its smaller relative the lesser spotted dogfish reaches a weight around the 4lb mark. The spur-dogfish is a much maligned fish which roves the sea in voracious packs to the great annoyance of boat anglers, who frequently up-anchor and shift marks rather than catch a never ending succession of these scavenging creatures. Spurdogs can attain the 20lb range and, like the greater and lesser spotted dogs, they are primarily fish eaters, but when they are hungry and assembled in large packs they will take anything which is edible. To avoid a series of bitten-off hooks when dogfish are around (provided of course that you have no objection to catching them) it is advisable to fit a pliable wire trace mounted hook to your terminal tackle to withstand their grinding teeth and sandpaper-like skin.

As a pleasant change from the mini-shark family, which are not considered by most sea angling gourmets as the last word in

131

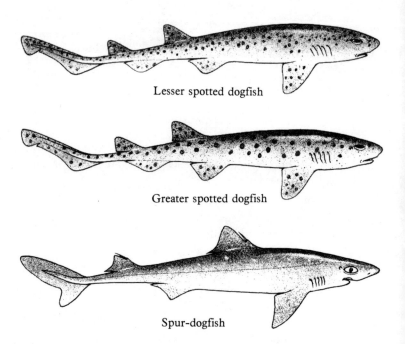

Lesser spotted dogfish

Greater spotted dogfish

Spur-dogfish

piscine delight, let us now consider those highly prized table fish species, the flatfish tribe, whose present-day price at the fishmongers occasions the rather rueful remark that 'They are strictly bottom feeders, but that description is exactly opposite to their price'. The flounder, the dab and the plaice continually gladden the hearts of pier fishermen, and small boys in particular, as they have an endearing habit of literally hanging themselves on to your tackle and then giving the rod end a series of twitches just to let you know they have hooked themselves. Together with the sole, which is a strictly nocturnal feeder with a very tiny mouth requiring the smallest of hooks to catch it successfully, these flatfish can be taken all around our shoreline. Sometimes they are found in just a few inches of water, especially over rich mud and sand bottoms which harbour worm and mussel beds and where there is a very gentle run of tide with no violently pounding wave action.

132

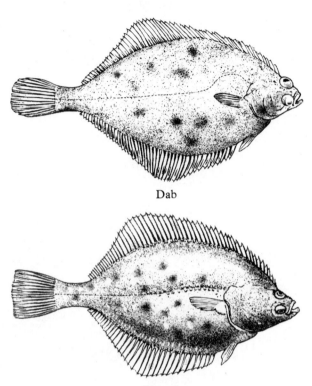

Dab

Flounder

Although flounders, dabs and soles can be taken in good sizes in inshore waters where the shorecaster's tackle can be operated, plaice in the larger sizes (and they are known to attain a weight of at least 8lb) are generally taken in much deeper offshore water by boat anglers. All the members of these flatfish species can be angled for with the lightest of shorefishing tackle, provided there are no snags and a very gentle run of tide. Calm, settled weather, with plenty of warm sun and clear water conditions, are the ideal times to take plaice, especially if they are being enticed to the baited hook with the addition of an attractor spoon incorporated into the terminal tackle set-up. This is bounced along the bottom to raise small puffs of sand and seems to titillate the curiosity of the plaice and cause it to chase after the moving bait.

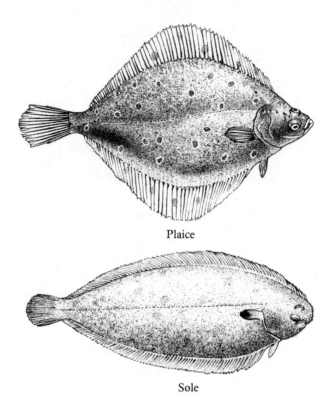

Plaice

Sole

There are two other species of flatfish which are usually caught in deep water by boat anglers, but at odd times are taken in shallow inshore waters by shorecasters. I refer, of course, to those twin culinary delights, the much sought after turbot and brill.

The members of the cod family make up quite a goodly selection of shorecaster's quarry fish, although two of them are considered to be primarily deepwater fish – the ling and the haddock – which are generally taken by boat anglers. Haddock do often feature in shore-caught catches, however, especially round the western parts of Scotland in the deeply indented sea lochs, from whose rocky shorelines casting can often be done into water deep enough to compare with fishing from a boat. That famous

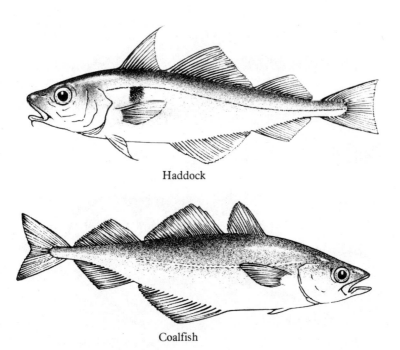

Haddock

Coalfish

deepwater wreck fish, the ling (which is often mistaken by people unfamiliar with it for a conger eel), has also been taken from the shore in its smaller sizes.

Coalfish, in the larger sizes, feature heavily in deepwater wreck fish catches. However, they are prolific all round the coast of the British Isles, especially in the North of England and around the whole of Scotland. On the Yorkshire coast they are known as 'billet' and delight small boys, who fish from harbour walls. Generally they favour rock and weed marks which give on to deep water.

Still with the cod family, let us consider that haunter of pinnacle rock marks and reefs, the pollack. Its feeding habits strongly resemble that ferocious freshwater predator, the pike. It is an ambush feeder, preferring to lurk in the cover of rocks and make sudden slashing attacks rather than chase its prey in open water. Great success can be had with pollack by spinning for

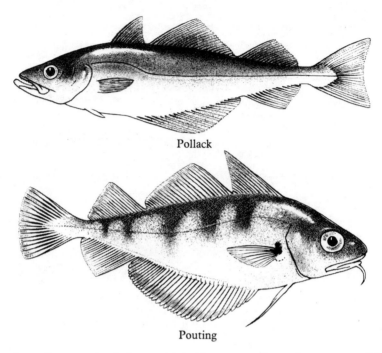

Pollack

Pouting

them from rocky ledges which give on to deep clear water. Of course, the size of such shore-caught pollack will in no way match those fish which can be taken from a boat over deepwater pinnacle rock. Big boat-caught pollack can reach a weight of around the 25lb mark but from the shore fish weighing into double figures can be encountered.

Pouting (or pout and pout-whiting) are apt to be regarded as a nuisance fish by discerning shorecasters who are after bigger, more delectable eating fish. The pout does, however, continually gladden the heart of the shorefishing matchman by affording him an easily caught weighty bag of fish to put on the scales at the end of the match. A 3lb shore-caught pouting is a very big one indeed. These fish can be located almost everywhere round our shoreline and they will take all baits avidly. So far as their eating qualities are concerned, a friend of mine just about sums up their culinary attributes in these few choice words: 'On their own, they

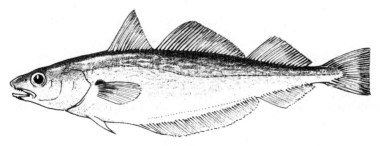

Whiting

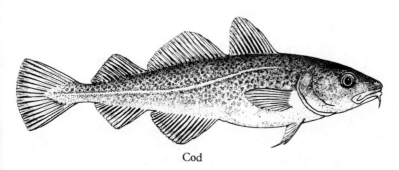

Cod

are shocking. But minced up with potato, seasoning and butter and fried in hot deep fat . . . they make passable fish cakes.' Incidentally, although the pouting is not a favourite part of the human diet, this fish in a size of about 1lb makes a wonderful whole hook offering for conger eels.

We are now about at the end of the cod family. There are just two fish left to consider: the whiting and the cod itself. Whiting have come to be known by shore anglers who fish the beaches in winter as the forerunner of the cod shoals. They move into shallow inshore water in reach of the beach and pier casters' tackle during the autumn and winter months, particularly during calm frosty weather. The whiting, with its mouth full of needle-sharp teeth and its voracious appetite, is a fish which is by no means a fussy feeder. Almost any type of bait will take whiting when they are feeding and shoaling in good numbers inshore. In their smaller sizes they are an everlasting curse of anglers hoping to catch bigger fish, as they strip the bait off large hooks with the utmost efficiency. From the shore a whiting of 3lb is a memorable fish. Their size over deepwater boat marks is much larger, 6lb being a noteworthy specimen, and they are known to reach a top weight of about 7 or 8lb. But fish of that size are usually taken by commercial netters.

In my estimation at least, to round off this appraisal of the cod family, I have saved the best till last: none other than that gaping mouthed, capacious stomached gobbler of anything edible, Old King Cod himself. Around this fish a world industry has grown up, and if sensible conservation measures are not practised to protect global cod stocks that very same industry will fall by the wayside, never to rise again. Some sea anglers (especially those living in areas which have a winter cod run from autumn to early spring) fish for nothing else. On the Yorkshire beach marks a whole army of after-dark anglers turn out with paraffin pressure lamps when the 'cod are in', but they quickly lose interest when these fish move offshore again about April and the demon bait-robbing crabs appear on the summer holiday beaches to make beachcasting quite intolerable.

Some really enormous cod have been taken by shorefishers— scores of fish in the 30 to 40lb weight bracket, topped off by a magnificent 44½lb specimen from Wales, a part of the country which is not really supposed to be 'big cod territory'. Of course, the cod attains a size much larger than that modest figure. Although the current boat record stands at 53lb, that is quite a diminutive weight when compared with a really enormous cod taken off the coast of America which weighed in at a little over 200lb. Right here in our own coastal waters cod of 70 and 80lb are regularly landed by trawlers.

The movements of cod have always been very unpredictable so far as the shorecaster is concerned. Some years are much better than others, with the smaller codling showing up off the beaches in the wake of the whiting as early as the end of September, and the bigger deepwater cod into double figures being taken in the coldest winter months. Sometimes, however, the winter cod run is very sparse indeed, with just a few odd, big deepwater cod appearing at what is known as the tail-end of the season around Easter time.

Until quite recently the western part of the English Channel and the Cornish coastal waters were not considered a cod-producing area. These waters, with their warm Atlantic influence, were supposed to be the wrong habitat for the cold-water-loving cod. Then in the early 1970s a great and perplexing change took place in the migrations of cod along the South coast, and at the present time cod are being caught all around that area. There are several explanations being given for this amazing happening. One is that the food fish of the cod are continually moving their shoaling grounds due to the disturbance of intensive commercial fishing. Another is that when an exceptionally good cod breeding year occurs, or even a series of such years, the cod shoals become so prolific that the millions of fish are forced to extend their feeding range further in order to survive.

In certain deepwater areas where the coastline is very rocky, with great beds of dense kelp, a smallish breed of what are known as 'native' or 'tangle' codling are present. These fish are resident there all the year round and they have a particularly dark red or greenish colouring which is quite unmistakable when you catch one. I am quite sure that the cod is capable of making a rapid colour change so that it can quickly adapt to the area into which it moves to feed. When fishing in certain estuaries I have noticed that part of the catch were very dark green or brown fish which had obviously been resident in the dark, muddy estuarine waters for some time. Conversely, odd fish taken at the same time were a much lighter, grey or light-green colour. Such fish, I am certain, had just run in from deep water and had not yet had time to adapt their coloration to correspond with their new, thick water surroundings. As an interesting sidelight on the truly enormous 'gobble anything' appetite of the cod, while I have been gutting trawl-caught fish, the following unusual objects have emerged: plastic spoons and cups, the head of an old paint brush, a ladies'

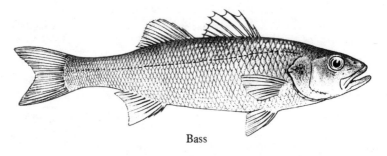

Bass

wooden shoe heel, part of a red industrial glove, and – most bizarre of all – the complete head and torso of a small vinyl doll!

I think it is quite true to say that, if the cod appeals to the majority of shorecasters as a weighty, easily caught quarry, with excellent 'freezer-filling' potential, that truly enigmatic fish, the bass, has such a romantic quality, both in appearance and habits, that there are sea anglers who concentrate on just this one species to the exclusion of all else. From the shore, the bass is a fish of wild, foamy, well oxygenated water and 'lonely sea and sky' beaches. To stand waist-deep in waders on a remote 'surf table' beach and cast light tackle far out into the shining foam is to some sea anglers the absolute pinnacle of angling bliss. Such devoted exponents of the art of white-water bassing do not expect to stagger away from the shoreline under a great weight of fish. Indeed, if they are fortunate enough to take quite a number of bass of a large takeable size, they do not greedily bang them on the head and retain the lot. Instead, with the conservation aspect uppermost in their minds, they sensibly return most of their catch and perhaps keep just a couple for the table.

A long time ago (fifty years to my personal knowledge) when trawling was in its heyday and fresh plaice, haddock and cod were cheap and plentiful, the bass was inclined to be a rather obscure fish, seldom seen in the fish markets and most certainly not in demand as a popular table fish. Today, alas, the scene has changed. Trawling is in decline through economic upheaval and over-fishing. Fish prices have rocketed to unprecedented levels, and with our entry into the EEC a great demand for almost any sea fish has been created in this country by French buyers. Sad to relate, we now have a situation where every small boat owner, who trails his craft to the coast most weekends, tucks under the thwarts a net of some description and uses it to good (I should say in the interests of fish conservation – *bad*) effect to line his pockets with cash or top up his deep freezer at home. The bass is an extremely slow-growing fish which takes a great many years to mature to full breeding size. The present minimum lawful takeable size limit of 12½in (32cm) introduced on 1 May 1981 is still far too low to ensure a continuation of the species. The new limit of 15in (38cm) which is proposed and scheduled for introduction from 1 May 1983 is also in my estimation still too small; 18in (46cm), or even better, 20in (51cm), would be a far more realistic figure for conservation to be effective.

I make absolutely no apologies for this rather lengthy digression, in the interests of fish stock conservation. Anyone reading this book will have a clear picture of the situation as it stands at the present time, and will not have his mind filled with rosy 'fairyland fiction', which is the painless palliative put forward by some devious politicians every time the subject of inshore and deepwater fishing is under review.

As the British Isles lies just within the most northerly limits of temperature range which the bass is capable of inhabiting, the South of England and especially the Atlantic side, the West Country, Wales and also Ireland, provide the most consistent bass fishing. However, there is a fair run of bass up the Yorkshire coast, but as very few anglers fish specially for them the reports in the angling press about bass catches from that area are naturally very few. Moreover, with the advent of modern power stations at various points around our coastline, which have immense warm water outflows into the sea, the patterns of fish migrations and coastal movements are apt to change almost overnight.

So far as big bass are concerned, I am quite sure that the shore-casters have just as much chance of hooking a monster as the boat fishers. The present boat and shore records for bass are held

Conger eel

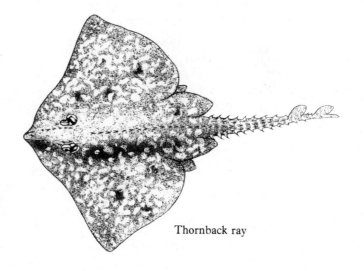
Thornback ray

by two fish both just over the 18lb mark. This by no means suggests that 18lb plus is the heaviest bass that can ever be taken. I have seen many bass of around the 20lb mark taken in gill nets and small trawls which ended up on the fishmonger's slab.

In sharp contrast to all the fish species we have considered previously in this chapter, the conger eel is in a category all on its own. For those adventure-seeking anglers who like a little danger to flavour their shorefishing and a worthy adversary that can fight just as well out of water as in, I would recommend conger fishing. What is more, just to make things even more interesting, the best time for conger catching is in the dark, and the most productive marks are a steep rocky shore giving onto deep water. Truly the conger eel is an accommodating species of sea fish. It is found all round our coastline in good numbers, especially over the most rocky, rough ground imaginable. Big conger are also known to inhabit harbours which do not dry out

A thornback ray taken by the author at dusk on a flat sandy beach, on lugworm. Note the thorny tail: a good reason for not diving your hand into the water to grab it as it is being landed. Use a gaff or wear thick, waterproof industrial gloves

A formidable Yorkshire rock mark, Filey Brig, showing the flat rock ledges. Studded footwear is essential here. It is extremely dangerous to fish this type of venue in rough weather or when a heavy ground swell is running which could produce freak or rogue waves at low tide and the tangled masses of ironwork and concrete which go to make up pier structures, jetties and breakwaters.

So far as size is concerned, it is true to say that the sky seems to be the limit. The present shore-caught record is a massive 67lb; from a boat the figure is 109lb. But these conger are mere infants to some reported washed up dead or caught in trawls; these monster conger have ranged right up to the 200–300lb mark. From a conservation point of view, I think the conger is in no danger. Its flesh is not very popular with the fish-fancying public, who seem to be put off eating it simply by the thought that it is more like a vast sea serpent than an edible fish.

The skate and ray family is also a very widely distributed species. But only a few skate are taken by shore anglers as this 'ton up' weight category fish is generally found on rough ground in deep water. Of the rays (which run to quite a number of different varieties) the thornback is the one most common around our coast. It is also the most edible from a fish and chips point of view.

Thornbacks are generally regarded as summer fish which come into the shallow waters on gently shelving sand and sand, mud and shingle beaches to do their courting and carry out their breeding rituals. Thornback fishing is a wonderfully relaxing, after-dark, summer style of angling. Warm breathless nights are best with a gentle neap tide just lapping in tiny wavelets on the beach. Lying back in comfort in a beach lounging chair, the thornback angler can gaze up at the starry sky and wait for the ratchet on his multiplier reel to give him an audible warning that a thornback ray has sampled his bait and is flapping away over the sea bottom with it. Of all the fish in the sea, and I have tried hundreds, the skinned wings of a thornback ray, fried to a crisp, golden brown in deep fat, are to me the most delectable sea food on earth.

Before leaving the skate and ray family, I consider it important that the shorecasting sea angler should have a very brief idea of what different species there are which may become attached to the end of his line, because at least three of the rays are highly dangerous customers to tangle with.

As previously stated, from a shore angling point of view, the skates can be dismissed altogether. Whilst a number of 100lb-plus fish have been taken by anglers fishing from Fenit pier, County Kerry in Ireland, such catches are not generally made elsewhere. Three distinct species of skate inhabit our waters: the white skate, the common skate and the long-nosed skate.

The rays present real difficulty so far as correct identification is concerned, as there is often a great variation in colour between the same species taken over different ground. Apart from the popular thornback ray, which attains a known size of 38lb (boat-caught) and half that weight from the shore, there is the blonde ray, small-eyed or painted ray, spotted or homelyn ray, undulate or pop-art ray, cuckoo ray, sandy ray, starry ray, shagreen ray, electric ray, and the extremely dangerous sting ray which has a lethal, venomous spike in its tail, which it lashes around when beached. The eagle ray also has a venomous sting in its whip-like tail and this fish should be treated with great caution. Any lacerations received from either of these venomous rays should warrant immediate hospital treatment for the unfortunate person who has fallen foul of them.

Finally a word about that novel creature, the electric ray, the boat record for which is a hefty 96lb with the shore-caught record weighing in at 48½lb. These fish are capable of giving a quite powerful electric shock to anyone handling them or standing on them (especially with bare feet). Their shocking equipment is situated on each side of the 'wings'. Let us hope that anyone taking one of these fish from the shoreline in the dark and nonchalantly plunging his hands into the foaming brine to heave it shorewards will be fortunate and take a fish with 'flat batteries'.

The mullet (of which there are four species in our waters) is truly a shorecaster's fish, as the current weight records will reveal. All those taken from the shore are well in excess of those hooked and landed from a boat. The thick-lipped grey mullet is the most common, and the one which attains the largest size; the

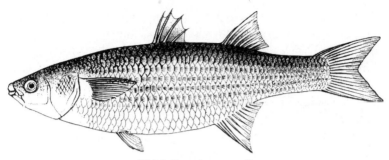
Thick-lipped grey mullet

boat record for this fish is just over 10lb, while the shore-caught record fish is a little over 14lb. The thin-lipped grey mullet does not grow so large; the shore-caught record is approximately 6lb and there is an open qualifying weight of 2lb for this species in the boat category. Two lesser known species are the rare golden-grey mullet and the red mullet (which, although called by that name, is actually a member of a different family).

An enormous amount of misconception flourishes in angling circles about the coastal distribution of the mullet. For years these fish were ruled to be a species which were only takeable in the southern areas of our coastline. That was in the unenlightened days when very few anglers fished for mullet and the fish were allowed to retain an image of being uncatchable. Recently a tremendous amount of interest has been generated within the ranks of serious sea anglers about mullet fishing. These wily creek, estuary, harbour and rivermouth-loving fish have been carefully studied and fished for on a scale previously undreamed of, by the very best of angling specimen hunters, using the lightest of coarse fishing tackle and a truly astounding variety of baits. As I have said, the old boat-caught record for a fish of just over 10lb taken in 1952 at Portland has been well topped by the fantastic 14lb-plus fish taken from near the Aberthaw Power Station on the Welsh coast. The amazing thing about this fish is its unbelievably rapid growth rate, due no doubt to the effect of living in a super-heated warm water environment, with an abundance of rich food growth in the surrounding area.

147

Anyone seeking to locate large mullet can do no better than to seek out a warm water outflow which is either right on the shoreline or even well up a river, as long as the mullet can have free access. Mullet are renowned as being scavengers pure and simple. My experience of them is that they will eat anything edible provided it is rather soft and mushy; the type of food is not particularly important. The outlets from canning factories, fish-processing plants and places where discarded table food is jettisoned into harbours, creeks and rivers are all places where mullet will congregate for a free feed. No matter how rotten or gruesome the stuff thrown into the water, or alternatively pumped into it from waste pipes, the mullet appear to love it and feed on it ravenously when the mood takes them. Mullet are capable of tolerating a water quality far below that of most sea or freshwater fish. They can be found up rather foul-looking creeks feeding on the most nauseating rubbish imaginable. Likewise, I have observed them quite happily taking floating bread in a harbour where the water surface was rainbow-coloured from a surface film of oil from the diesel engines of many moored drifters.

The wrasse family are a group of crab-crunching, shellfish-eating, rock-loving fish which are widely distributed around all rock-bound shorelines, particularly on the South coast, with the emphasis on the Cornish coastline with its indented rocky gullies and caverns. Altogether there are seven species of wrasse, but only the two largest, the ballan and the cuckoo, reach an appreciable size worthy of being seriously angled for. The boat records are 7½lb for the ballan and 2lb for the cuckoo, while the shore-caught figures are 8lb-plus for the ballan and 1lb 9oz for the cuckoo.

Wrasse are not considered to be a table fish by the majority of sea anglers, but in the Channel Islands they have a recipe for baked wrasse which I am told is quite palatable. The feeding habits of wrasse are very convenient for the wellbeing of shore anglers; they just love warm, settled weather conditions.

To round off this chapter I have purposely left until last two

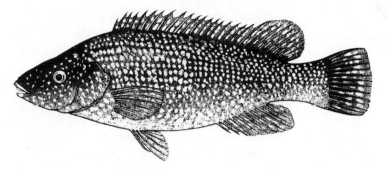

Ballan wrasse

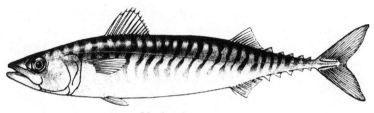

Mackerel

Garfish

very sporting (but not very large) surface feeding fish which will provide endless thrills if they are angled for with appropriate light tackle. The mackerel and the garfish are both upper water predators which can be taken on a variety of baits, spinners and lures. Many years ago it would have been quite correct, when writing of the mackerel, to say that each summer they came close inshore in massive shoals. But they no longer assemble by the million around headlands and in bays; commercial fishing has so depleted the stocks that in some years, around certain areas, they do not appear at all.

The boat fishing record for garfish is nearly 3lb with the shore record almost the same weight, plus a couple of ounces.

Mackerel are somewhat heavier. The boat record is almost 5½lb and the shore one 4lb and a few drams. Every year when the mackerel are shoaling around certain points, I am horrified to see supposed 'sportsmen' landing them by the half dozen on powerful tackle armed with a barbaric string of what are called 'mackerel feathers'. Such a method of angling, from a boat, in order to fill the bait box is a possible way of taking them, when these fish are required for a hook offering for bigger species: sharks, conger, skate and such heavyweight species which love a fresh mackerel, whole or filleted. But mackerel and garfish give a wonderful account of themselves if they are taken on sensibly balanced light tackle. It is wasteful and disgusting to haul such fish out in strings on heavy gear and take far more than can be comfortably carried away, leaving the residue to rot on the rocks or quayside in the sun, thereby offending non-anglers and bringing our sport into disrepute.

11
Successful Methods, Rigs and Bait

Having gone deeply, in the preceding chapters, into the subject of tackle, baits, locations, and the type of fish which are to be caught, not forgetting of course, how they react to different weather conditions and the state of their natural environment, the sea, now comes the shore angler's moment of truth – how to put together all this knowledge and relate it to the catching of some fish. I will freely admit that the aptitude for being in the right place, at the best time, to present a suitable bait to a fish which is in a feeding mood, and then to hook, play and land it successfully, is what distinguishes accomplished sea anglers from the 'cast out and hope for a miracle' operators.

First let us consider what I will term the classic beachcasting situation which is to be met all round our coastline – where heavy tackle is used to combat a strong, lateral tide flow over a steep or flat shelving beach, and the catch is primarily winter cod up to low double figures (say 2–about 20lb), small whiting, flatfish, dogfish, spurdogs, rays during the summer months, and the occasional tope or bass, according to geographical location. At the outset, let me stress that the tackle employed in such angling situations is always geared to beat the fishing conditions rather than the fish. A powerful beachcaster in the region of 10–12ft is therefore suitable, coupled with the reel of your choice, which could be a multiplier, a big fixed-spool reel or a side-cast. Unless the shoreline is really snag-free, the main reel line should be over 20lb b.s., and preferably about 25–30lb. If a light line is used to combat a strong tide on a very kind beach where no tackle will be lost, a strong casting piece is still necessary so that 'crack-offs' are minimised.

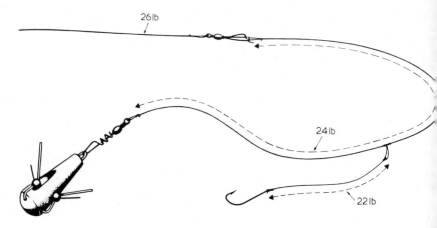

Beachcasting terminal rig — paternoster

The best terminal tackles for all kinds of shorefishing are those which are simple, tangle-free and do not incorporate any useless accoutrements. Booms, beads and lots of swivels make tackle losses prohibitively expensive, as well as adding air resistance which will cut down your casting distance. To the end of my main reel line, I tie a quick release swivel. Below that I add a 3ft length of lower breaking strain line with a blood-dropper loop in the middle. The bottom end of this piece of nylon monofil has a swivelled corkscrew lead-link attached to it, so that various weights of 'breakaway' leads can easily be changed to suit the tidal flow. From the blood-dropper loop, a short hook snood is fixed, of a lower breaking strain than the lead to reel line link. This completes the terminal rig known as the paternoster: reel line, say, 26lb; quick release swivel to lead link 24lb; hook snood 22lb, thereby giving a reduced breaking strain terminal tackle which will not cause a loss of reel line if the lead or hook becomes snagged.

It is vital for your own safety and that of other shore users that the sinker is never attached direct to the nylon monofilament line of your terminal tackle. The reason for this precaution is that, when the tackle is being reeled in over sand, shingle and stones, the attachment immediately above the lead loop gets a great deal

152

of wear from being pulled through abrasive sand and sharp stones. If it is nylon line, it will be very rapidly weakened and on the next cast the lead is liable to 'crack-off'. A quick release 'cork-screw' lead link made of stout brass wire which incorporates a good quality swivel will totally safeguard the slightest chance of a flying lead.

Although long casting in such shorecasting situations as we are now considering is often of great advantage for catching fish, certain indisputable facts will emerge when the angler has a wide experience of beach fishing in strong tides with heavy tackle and 'grapple' leads. I find when I cast a distance exceeding 100 yards that the stretch of the line, and the 'belly' in it caused by the tide, nullifies any violent striking motions I may make with the rod in an attempt to hook a fish, unless, when I see a bite signalled on the rod tip, I take a few paces backwards and tighten up the line to the sinker by reeling in a few yards. When fishing at a greater range than 100 yards with a 'grapple' lead, I find that the fish usually grabs the bait hastily and is brought up sharp by the resistance of the lead anchored to the bottom. When the angler sees a 'bite' on his rod tip, as it bounces violently, what he is really watching is the fish struggling after it has been hooked automatically by the anchored tackle. Any movements which he makes with the rod usually drive the hook more firmly home. I am certain, however, that sometimes when the angler strikes violently at a fish, far from hooking it, he pulls the hook out, especially if the fish, on grabbing the bait and attempting to swim away with it, has only lightly hooked itself against the resistance of the wired lead.

When a monopod is used on a beach with the rod mounted as far above the wave action as possible so that the line is clear of the breaking waves, two distinct types of bite will be signalled on the rod tip. One is usually a violent dithering of the tip, and sometimes, with a big fish, this is followed by the rod tip being pulled down hard into a good bend. Conversely, quite often the taut line from rod tip to lead will suddenly fall slack and the rod straighten up in its rest. These two bite indications are the ones most commonly met in heavy beach fishing. The first type indicates that the fish has sampled the bait and is moving away from the angler. The second, known as a 'slack line bite', is when the fish takes the bait (often being hooked in the process) and swims rapidly inshore towards the angler.

When fishing at extreme casting range, two immediate difficulties will be experienced. One is the failure of very soft baits to withstand really hard casting, and the other is getting the hook to penetrate the mouth of the fish when there is a great distance between the man with the rod and the biting fish. Some fanatical long distance casters actually limit their bait selection to hook offerings which are very tough and, in order to gain even more distance, they foolishly cut down their bait size and length of hook snood to give the most streamlined terminal tackle possible. Such addled thinking is the wrong approach to fish catching. Why strain your tackle and every muscle in your body to belt out a sinker 150 yards plus and then, when the terminal tackle splashes down among the fish, waste all that superhuman effort because the hook offering is a miserable scrap of bait which, although it is as tough as boot leather, has no appeal to the fish?

That very popular bait, the lugworm, will stand hard casting if it is carefully threaded on the hook head first and then locked into position by a piece of tough squid or razorfish mounted on the bend and point of the hook. Mussel and lugworm cocktail will also stay on the hook very well if the mussels are mounted first, as described earlier, in the chapter on baits, and this offering is irresistible to foraging cod when the water is well churned up just before or after a spell of rough weather.

The problem of hooking fish at extreme casting range – 100 yards plus – is quite a knotty one which I have been unable to solve in all my years of experience on the tideline. Two factors must be taken into consideration when grappling with this problem. A strong, forged hook with a large barb will land a big fish once it is securely hooked; but such a hook will require an enormous amount of striking power to drive the point into the mouth of the fish well past the barb in order to give a secure hookhold. Conversely, a fine, round wire hook with a small barb quite near the hook point is easily driven into the mouth of the fish. However, should the fish be very large and of a species which twists and rolls once you have it on a short line in a powerful run of surf just prior to hauling it up the beach, then the chances of either the hook breaking under the strain or pulling out are very high. Whatever hook pattern you finally choose for the particular type of fish catching you are concentrating on, do remember that your chances of hooking and holding your catch will be improved 50 per cent if you carry around in your pocket a small sliver of fine carborundum stone and periodically (whilst fishing) check your hook point and sharpen it up whenever necessary.

The knots you tie in your beachcasting terminal tackle, and particularly the one used to join your strong casting leader to your main reel line, are vital links which really decide the strength of your tackle. Some knots are quite wrong in construction for use in nylon line. In addition, the correct knots need to be tied properly and tensioned correctly so that the line does not lose a great percentage of its breaking strain poundage. For many years I relied on the bloodknot—both the double and the single, or 'half', one in its 'tucked' form—for tying leader knots and eyed hooks. Then a few years ago I was introduced to the single and double 'grinner' knot, and found it so vastly superior to my old faithful bloodknots that I was instantly converted to its use. The double and single 'grinner', together with the double overhand loop, the blood loop and the spade end knot are all tried and trusted knots for making up terminal tackles and tying on hooks.

The correct way to tie knots in nylon monofilament line, to ensure that it retains the highest degree possible of its original breaking strain and the knots do not 'creep' or slip, is as follows. First moisten the part of the line to be knotted either by immersing it in water or running it between your lips to give it a good coating of saliva. Next form the knot and make sure the

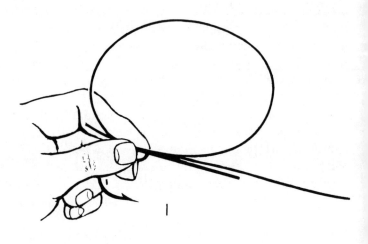

1

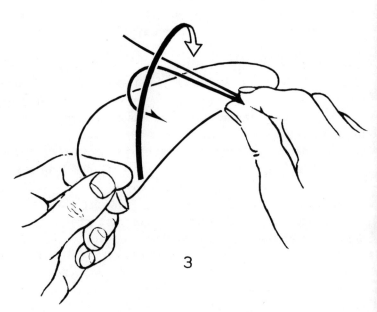

3

Tying the spade end knot

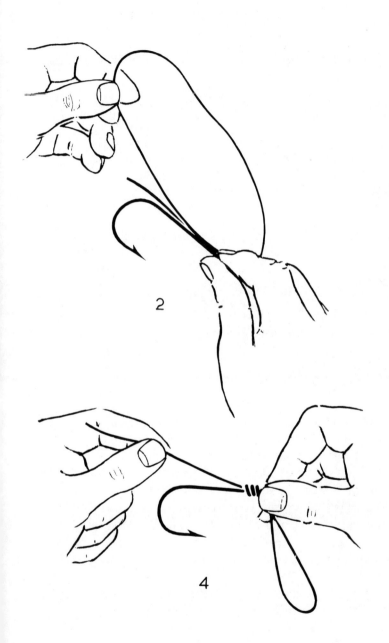

2

4

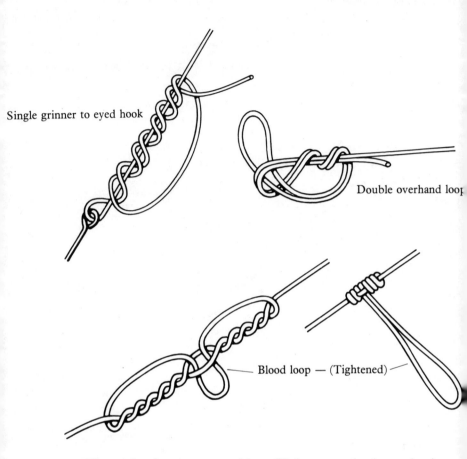

Single grinner to eyed hook

Double overhand loop

Blood loop — (Tightened)

coils are in the proper position. Tighten up the knot slowly, watching that it beds down correctly and the coils are snugged down and evenly formed. Finally, give it a good testing by pulling it steadily, and then examine the knot itself and the line near it for distortion, stress marks or twisting. If in doubt about the performance of the knot under fishing stress, cut the line and tie another one. Failure to do so may lose you the fish of a lifetime or, worse still, bury your 6oz bullet-shaped lead in the skull of your best friend.

Recently, a new type of spear spade hook has appeared on the tackle market which is specifically designed to assist the angler in

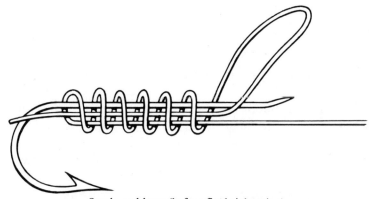

Spade end knot (before final tightening)

mounting soft baits so that they remain in position. I find that spade end hooks, which have the end of the shank flattened where the eye on a normal hook is situated, are very good for mounting baits which should not be mangled if they are slotted up the hook shank a little way. The new spear spade hooks are quite strong, yet fine in the wire and particularly suitable for worm baits or mounting soft crabs. Baitholder hooks, which have sliced barbed shanks, are also very good for retaining worm baits in position when vigorous casting is being done. There is one drawback to their design, however, which I find most off-putting. Because the hook shanks have to be deeply cut in the manufacturing process so that the bait-retaining barbs can be raised, these hooks are usually made far too thick in the wire for my liking.

Some species of fish with powerful grinding teeth like the members of the ray family, or others such as the tope which have a line-chafing skin as well, will quickly make short work of a normal nylon monofilament hook snood and swim off with the angler's hook in their jaws. To obviate this annoying happening, and ensure that within reason all fish that are hooked are successfully landed, specially strong terminal tackles should be used for tope, rays and certain members of the dogfish tribe.

Since rays do not take kindly to stiff wire traces attached to the hook (they find them uncomfortable when they flop down upon the bait and immediately become suspicious), a hook snood of 60 or 70lb breaking strain commercial fishing nylon can be used and is strong enough to withstand the crunching of their shellfish-grinding molars. Tope are a different proposition. The trace for these shark-type fish must be at least 6ft long and made of cable laid wire, and should have a couple of weight-tested, high quality swivels incorporated into its length. The reason for the long trace will be seen when a tope is hooked in shallow water. It will often roll or twist itself in the trace wire, which of course will withstand such harsh treatment. Were the trace made up from ordinary nylon, or even heavy duty commercial nylon monofil, the rough skin of the tope would soon make short work of it, if its razor sharp teeth had not already done so.

There are two separate schools of thought on the best kind of terminal tackle to be used for heavy beachcasting. The old established anglers mostly prefer the paternoster rig, where the lead hangs at the bottom of the set-up and the hook snood is suspended from a blood loop a short distance up the line. The running leger rig is quite different. Here, the hook hangs down at the bottom of the rig and the sinker or casting weight is threaded on to the main reel line through its attachment loop and then stopped by a barrel swivel, one ring of which takes the reel line, the other the hook trace.

Both these terminal rigs have good and bad points. I find that the paternoster type automatically hooks lots of fish which do not show up a distinct bite indication on the rod tip, especially in situations where there is a strong tidal flow or if the wind makes bite detection difficult. On the other hand, a minus factor for this rig is the fact that when a good fish is hooked, which dives powerfully for the bottom, it is often aided in its attempt to rid itself of the hook by the trailing lead becoming caught up in the rocks or stony bottom and snagging weed growth. The running leger terminal tackle obviates this last drawback. With the lead mounted above the hook, when a fish is being brought shorewards, the lead rides higher up in the water and does not trail;

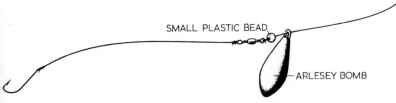

SMALL PLASTIC BEAD

ARLESEY BOMB

Running leger

snagging is therefore almost completely eliminated. In theory, the running leger should allow a fish to move off with the bait without feeling any resistance from the lead because the line can be pulled freely through the eye on which the lead is attached. This is a good point if it works that way. What usually happens, however, is that the line is twisted around the lead loop attachment and the fish hooks itself against the weight of the sinker, particularly if it is fitted with 'grapple' wires. Instead of the line running freely through the sinker loop, it is firmly tangled in it so that instead of the bite showing up on the rod tip, as it would with the paternoster rig where the reel line has the hook snood mounted above the lead, the running leger or flowing trace terminal tackle allows the fish to pull against the anchored lead and these movements are not always transmitted up the line to the rod tip.

A killing livebaiting technique can be practised from beaches and also piers and harbour walls, when there are plenty of small whiting and pouting about which are proving to be a bait-stealing nuisance as they grab baits which are intended for large cod. Mount two hooks on your terminal tackle, one small, about size 1/0, and another bigger one about size 6/0 three or four inches above it. Bait both hooks with lugworm, razorfish, mussel, or a cocktail of all three. After casting out your twin hook rig, two things may happen. If you are in luck, a big cod will gulp down the whole works and be firmly hooked and bring you great joy when it is landed. Alternatively, a small whiting or pouting may become hooked on the smaller bait and rattle your rod tip in the characteristic small fish manner. At this point in the proceedings, it is essential that you exercise great self-control and the utmost

161

patience. What you are doing now is fishing at range with a tethered livebait on your terminal gear. This is the only way I know to do it. You cannot cast a live fish far, and even if you could, the flight through the air and the shock of hitting the sea would kill it. This alternative method most certainly works; you do not take a whole string of fish, but what you do catch usually make up for their sparseness by their size.

A variation on this livebaiting technique can be worked from high rock marks or piers, jetties and harbour walls. It is called the 'slide-down' method and relies for its efficiency on the angle of the line from rod tip to sinker being quite steep. Basically, it is used where small live fish can easily be caught with a light rod at the same fishing position as the heavy gear is to be operated from. First procure the live baits and keep them in good trim in a suspended coarse fishing keepnet or a bucket with a battery-driven aerator pump. Cast out the heavy tackle with just the sinker on the end of the line and some form of 'stop' fixed on the reel line at the distance above it where the live bait is to be presented. After the line has been tightened from rod tip to sinker and the rod has been rested securely against the harbour wall, pier rail or on a firm tripod, the livebaited drop-down tackle is prepared. This takes the form of a large hook (say, size 4/0 or 6/0) with the live fish lip-hooked, attached to a 3ft snood terminated by a quick release 'snap' or American (safety pin) swivel. This swivel is clipped on to the reel line and the bait allowed to slide down into position near the sinker on the bottom. For this tackle to work properly it is essential that there is not a strong wind blowing and that the surface of the water is not rough. It will facilitate a smooth 'slide', if some weight in the form of a small lead sinker is attached to the sliding livebait link.

Either of these livebait methods will certainly sort out the big fish from the tiddlers and bring a few rodbenders to the astute angler who is prepared to spend a little time and effort on trying it out. Cod are not the only fish which respond to a small live fish tethered to a leaded terminal tackle, and struggling violently to free itself. Big, solitary roving bass find such a meal very much to

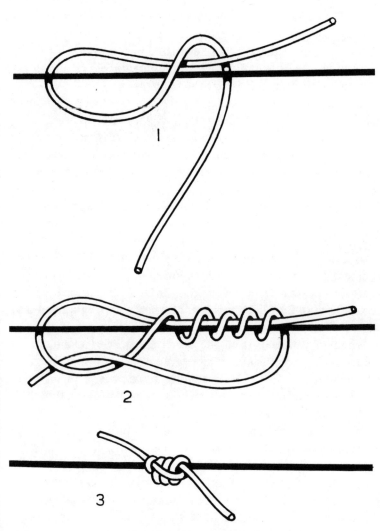

1

2

3

Sliding nylon stop knot

their liking. As also do large conger, especially if the method is operated at dusk over very rocky ground or immediately adjacent to a tangle of weed and barnacle-crusted pier supports, or in the vicinity of a harbour wall which is composed of enormous blocks of stone with deep crevasses in it.

In the interests of tackle safety, let me give a brief word of warning about leaving rods unattended with reels 'in gear', when fishing for species which are quite powerful. It is vital, if you do not wish to see your treasured tackle suddenly dive seawards, that the rod is securely positioned in an efficient rest and the reel is 'out of gear' with only the ratchet mechanism engaged. This will give just sufficient retardation of the spool to prevent the pull of the tide stripping off line if the terminal tackle shifts its position. When a large fish does grab the bait and swim off with it at a great pace, even if the angler has his back turned or is momentarily engaged in availing himself of his creature comforts (flasks, pipe, cigarettes or food), the audible clicking of the ratchet giving line will warn him of what is happening and also save his rod from being dragged into the sea.

When tope fishing from the beach or rocky headlands, it is essential that a reel is used which will carry a sufficient length of line to allow this fish to make its long initial runs. The main reel line for tope fishing need not be enormously strong; 20 to 30lb will be quite adequate, provided the terminal tackle incorporates at least 6ft of wire and a large 6/0 or 8/0 hook which is needle sharp. Whole or half mackerel and small tender-fleshed dabs are a favourite tope bait. When a tope picks up this type of bait it will usually make a very short fast run of a second or two, then pause to turn the bait in its mouth, preparatory to swallowing it. Then it will move off again. The start of its second short run is when the strike should be made, after which, if it is firmly hooked, all hell will appear to break loose as the tope goes off on its first long searing run. This is the time when the reel should be 'in gear' but with the star drag set very lightly, just enough to prevent the reel over-running. The first long run of a tope will strip anything up to 200 yards of line off your reel so, in the

164

interests of having a safety margin of line still left on the reel, at least 300 yards needs to be on the spool before you even attempt to tangle with a tope. No matter how powerful your tackle, it is the height of folly to attempt to stop a tope when it is making that first long fast run just after it has been hooked. Let it run against a minimum of spool drag so that it tires itself by pulling a long length of line against the resistance of the water.

To the consternation of the angler who is new to tope fishing, when he does retrieve some line and get the fish close to his angling position, it will most probably set off on a further series of runs which are apt to convince him that the fish is a demon which will never lose its stamina and energy. Nothing could be further from the truth. Be patient; play a cool, waiting game, retrieving line when possible and giving it back, until the fish finally tires itself out. Never try heavy-handed bullying tactics with tope. They are very fast, powerful fish which demand respect. Play them properly in a sensible manner and you will land them; give them the rough-stuff treatment and they will snap your line like cotton and make off with a hook stuck in their jaw and a wire trace with yards of trailing line.

After that brief excursion into the realms of the poor man's big game fishing, let us now consider what fish can be caught from jetties, piers, harbour walls and steep rock marks which have a good depth of water below them; at the same time giving some thought to the most suitable tackle and baits for fishing from these raised deepwater venues.

One immediate problem which presents itself to all anglers fishing from high vantage points is that of how to get a weighty fish up to the raised fishing position when you have hooked it. This is a knotty problem which should be faced long before the fish is thrashing around perhaps twenty or thirty feet below the angler, whose brain is working overtime trying to come up with a speedy solution. Basically, there are at least three or four recognised techniques to overcome this sticky situation and some are far better than others. The most obvious, but not the best, answer is to fish with tackle which is powerful enough to winch up the fish through the air. That is the theory on which Scarborough tackle works, but quite a lot of good fish are lost when the fish kicks violently and the hook tears out of its mouth.

Some very daring and often foolhardy anglers work in pairs when fishing rock marks. While the one with the rod holds the fish on the water surface, his rock-scrambling companion descends to the water level and either gaffs the fish or scoops it up in a strong landing net. All good adventurous, breathtaking stuff, if nothing goes wrong; unfortunately, in such situations, footholds can slip and big waves wash anglers off slimy rocks. Personally I don't think a fish, however large, is worth a drowned fishing friend.

On piers and harbour walls a 'drop-net' is the best answer to the big fish problem. Some piers, where the angling is well controlled and efficiently organised, actually sport a 'resident drop-net', usually of mammoth proportions which would comfortably haul up a fully grown angler if he fell into the drink. In the absence of a common property drop-net, each angler is advised to carry his own around. They can be bought in all sizes (and qualities) from good tackle shops. I will now pass on a time-honoured tip which will save many a lost drop-net if it is noted and acted upon. Immediately you buy your drop-net with long hauling line attached, get a fishing net cork (or one of the new-fangled plastic floats which have replaced the natural thing) and attach it to 'your end' of the net rope. Then when you eventually drop 'your end' of the rope into the water whilst using the net (and I am sure you will sometime or other) the rope floats with its attached cork and you can cast your tackle over it and retrieve your lost drop-net.

Drop-netting is a fine art. Especially if you are trying to net a large fish with a strong tide running and a lumpy sea breaking around the pier supports or along the harbour wall. On your own, with rod in one hand and drop-net rope in the other, you don't stand a ghost of a chance of netting your fish. If you possibly can, shout for help from another angler, and if he does not know the drill, give him a rapid teach-in on the spot whilst playing the fish so that he does not make a mess of the job. All the netsman does is to make sure that the drop-net is kept in a steady downtide position of the fish just under the surface. The angler with the rod then plays the fish to a standstill, brings it up to the surface uptide of the net, and literally guides it right over the net mouth so that when the netsman sees the fish over his net, he just hauls it up. In the dark the job is almost impossible and this is where a good headlight with a strong beam will prove its worth.

If you do get caught out totally alone on a pier at night, there is only one method I know of landing a heavy fish, apart from walking it all the way back to the shoreline to beach it or going down some steps to the water level. Tie the net rope to the pier handrail so that the net is suspended downtide of your angling position with the hoop just under the surface. When a big fish comes along, your only hope then of landing it is to manoeuvre it into the net, keep the line fairly tight on it, and then hurriedly haul on the rope to bring the fish and the net safely up to the pier decking—a job which I have done with difficulty and lost many a good fish when I have made the slightest mistake. The golden rule for drop-netting is: the person with the net must hold the net steady so that the angler can guide the fish into it. Any attempt on the part of the drop-net operator to 'chase after' a fish with the net will result in a lost fish. What usually happens is that the drop-netter lets the net sink low in the water with the intention of suddenly heaving it to the surface under the fish. Sometimes it works, but not often. Invariably the fish makes a sudden dive for freedom when it sees the net and the reel line gets tangled up with the drop-net rope with the fish still outside the net. Then the netsman panics and tries to haul the whole works out of the water, drop-net and tangled reel line, with the fish dangling below. Half way up the pier wall, the fish struggles violently, the hook pulls out, and the man with the rod threatens to throw the drop-net artist into the sea after the escaped fish. Pier fishing is often great entertainment—provided you are an onlooker!

I would advise all pier and rock-mark anglers to err on the long side when choosing a rod for such locations. As previously stated, a sound, heavy duty beachcaster with a foot or two lopped off the bottom makes a wonderful rock-mark and pier rod. The length is a great asset when a good fish has to be guided around snags or kept clear of barnacle-encrusted girders or wooden supports.

Long casting from piers and rock marks which have a good depth of water under them is seldom necessary. This immediately gives the angler two enormous advantages. His terminal tackle does not have to be streamlined; also, he can fish with large, bulky, soft baits, which would not be advisable if he was casting them hard from a beach position. An enormous variety of fish are regularly caught from piers and deepwater rock marks, and the angler who varies his tackle, methods and baits will find that his catches far outweigh those that are taken by the one-method, one-bait operators.

For flatfish, the traditional three-boom paternoster rig with short snoods and small hooks (2 or 4 freshwater size) can bring good results as the three hooks can hold a trio of different baits: lugworm, ragworm and mussel; small peeler crab, razorfish and live shrimp; squid tentacle, mackerel strip, and live sandeel. Although lug and ragworm are the generally accepted flatfish baits, it pays to experiment and not become hidebound in your bait choice. All the flatfish species are predatory and will chase after live baits. Therefore a top hook paternostered livebait offering, fished three or four feet off the sea bed, will often bring a steady succession of bites, while the other two hooks further down with different bait remain untouched.

Some piers and rock marks produce very big cod, but in very small numbers. These venues may also have resident shoals of whiting, pouting, 'strap' conger and flatfish. We have here the classic example of an everlasting dilemma: whether to fish with small hooks and appropriate tiny baits so that the action is fast and furious, or to put out a very big bait on a correspondingly large hook and sit tight with great patience and wait for a rodbending cod. While I do not generally advocate the use of two rods, this is one occasion when I would try two sets of tackle: a cod rod with a 6/0 hook and a liberal helping of lugworm on it, and also a small-fish rod with a three-boom paternoster rig, in the hope of some pan-sized flatfish and a decent whiting or two.

What usually happens is that the big cod, when it comes along, eagerly snaffles one of the baits intended for the small fish, is successfully hooked, delicately played and drop-netted on the small fish rod. Meanwhile, a 2lb flounder or plaice lies doggo on the bottom and somehow manages to engulf the huge cod bait on its 6/0 'meat hook', to be hauled up without any bite indication being shown on the rod tip when the gear is pulled in for a periodic bait check. Such are the vagaries of sea angling. Every summer we have holiday anglers, fishing with light tackle and dab hooks, landing outsize bass. The dyed-in-the-wool bass experts fish long and hard with all the right tackle and first-class bait and end some of their sessions either completely fishless or with the odd fryable flattie to save them from ridicule when they return home wet and worn out.

Congering from harbour walls and steep rock marks is definitely a lively form of angling, particularly if you can manage to do some all-night sessions when the big eels leave their daytime lying-up places and roam around over open ground and even ascend to mid-water in their hunt for food.

The tackle for shore congering need not be in the category of big shark strength. But it should be well balanced and of adequate power to lift the eels rapidly from the rocky bottom and keep them from diving into their funk holes, from which they cannot be removed, even if you employ a mobile crane. Although the record shore-caught conger scaled a truly massive 67lb 1oz, the usual size of exceptionally big eels from the shore runs to a top weight of about 40 to 50lb, with plenty of 'straps' in the 5 to 10lb weight range to give the shore conger artist some practice for the time when he hooks a real underwater snake. I recommend a powerful 12ft beachcaster for shore congering in conjunction with a wide-drummed multiplier reel carrying at least 300 yards of 35lb line. Do not get the wrong impression with regard to the length of the line. I am not expecting the conger to run out seawards like a tope and strip all the line off the reel drum. The 300 yards of line is an insurance against hooking one or two eels which are unstoppable. They usually get their tails around a big rock and prove to be immovable. All the angler can do then is to pull for a break with the line wrapped well round his coat sleeve to avoid cutting his hands, put on a new terminal tackle and start fishing again. Two or three episodes of that nature in the course of a night on the rocks after conger eels and you are down to the last 100 yards of reel line.

Conger tackle must be powerful, but never coarse or clumsy. The smallest possible weight should be used which will allow the tackle to remain stationary on the bottom. Conger sometimes nose around the bait for ages and are very delicate in their approach when they do decide to sample it. A sound cable-laid 18in wire trace of about 60lb breaking strain with a strong, forged, needle-sharp hook about size 6/0 or 8/0 is the ideal end tackle for conger. The swivel which joins the wire trace to the reel line must be of the quick-release pattern and weight tested so that the angler can know for a surety that it will withstand a greater stress than both line and wire trace. If the lead is mounted just above the wire trace and stopped by the quick release swivel, there will be nothing dangling free on the terminal tackle when the eel makes its bid for freedom and tries to regain the security of its rocky hiding place. The quick release swivel is to facilitate the angler, when he brings the conger ashore, quickly dropping it into a large sack, unclipping the hook trace, tying the mouth of the sack to prevent the eel escaping, and mounting another trace complete with hook offering on his tackle. He can be fishing again with the minimum of delay.

As I said in a previous chapter, whole small pouting or a mackerel head with the entrails dangling in a bloody, gooey mess are the baits for conger. Although eels are supposed to be seabed scavengers, big conger do prefer really fresh baits. Old, stale or freezer baits are not half as effective as fresh-from-the-sea fish baits with the body juices and blood oozing out and spreading a fish-attracting smear into the water.

170

A big, lively shore-caught conger eel will most certainly not allow itself to be scooped up into a landing net, no matter how large it is and how skilful the operator may be. A needle-sharp gaff which is both large and strong is the only type of landing gear for conger. If the rocks are steep and slippery and the eel is lively and large, then you have all the makings of a genuine, primitive, man-against-beast tussle. Shore angling can provide high adventure to suit all tastes, especially if the angler-versus-eel match is taking place in the dark!

One of the most skilful and rewarding (big fish-wise) facets of the whole shore-angling scene is, to use my personal description, light surfcasting tackle specimen hunting. For those very selective anglers, whose one aim in life is to take certain species of fish in their largest sizes, this kind of angling will definitely give them all the piscatorial fulfilment they desire.

Let me first give a description of the tackle I have in mind for this kind of angling. The rod is known as a bass rod or light surfcaster which is designed to cast a weight of 1–3oz and handle lines in the 10–20lb breaking strain category. Either a medium-sized multiplier or a small sea-size fixed-spool reel can be used in conjunction with the rod described. The terminal tackles, baits and angling techniques that can be employed with this set-up are innumerable, but I will do my best to list quite a few which I have found successful in a wide variety of shorecasting situations.

First and always exhilarating is 'Ye Olde Established Atlantic Storm' bass beach angling, in lively surf with three or four steady, regular water tables running in over a flat, sandy beach which allows safe, deep wading. Pride of location for this type of surf angling must go to those shining strands in Cornwall, Wales and certain parts of Ireland which have long been known to dedicated bass anglers, some of whom visit them on a fishing pilgrimage year after year.

To carry out this kind of fishing successfully, the bare minimum of tackle is required, as most of the time spent on the beach will be in the water waist-deep in breast waders. Therefore all tackle needed should be carried in pockets or a kind of kangaroo pouch suspended from the neck which fits neatly inside the front of the waders. Bait can be in a lidded plastic bucket (a small one for preference) which hangs from a belt loop on a quick-release dog-lead type of fastening.

In this situation, when the angler is deep wading, none of those fancy tournament-style casts can be executed, particularly not those which demand a very long down drop from rod end to sinker nor the South African cast which begins with the terminal tackle laid out on the beach. I find that the only cast which is suitable when wading with the water about waist high is a modified version of the layback cast. However, the rod will have to be held a little higher and the casting arc can in no way be as long as that when the cast is made on dry land.

Surf-table fishing does not generally require long casting so much as really accurate casting. The tackle must be placed where the bass are feeding, and sometimes this is only a short way from where the angler is actually standing. Frequently I have stood in the surf and on looking back shorewards seen large bass furrowing their way behind me, literally in mere inches of foamy water.

The terminal tackles for this white water bass fishing can be of the simplest kind imaginable. I find just two types will suffice — the single hook paternoster and the running leger — since the heavy scouring which the last few yards of line will receive in the surf, with its coarse sand or shingle bottom, will play havoc with a reel line about 15lb breaking strain. On this occasion a strong casting piece of about 30lb will be advisable. For either tackle set-up, a selection of plain bombs and also 'breakaways' will be necessary in weights between 1 and 3oz. It is essential, if the greatest possible sport is to be got from the fish caught, that they have the barest weight of lead hampering them. A lead which will just give enough casting weight and also hold bottom is the one to use.

Baits for this kind of surf strand fishing can be either lug or ragworm with razorfish and clams as a second line of attack.

Sometimes a cocktail mixture of worm and shellfish will tempt the bass better than a single bait. I like fine wired hooks about size 2/0 to 3/0 with the points honed needle sharp and frequently checked for sharpness during the fishing sessions. On a beach with stones the hook point should be checked after each retrieve.

This same kind of light surfcasting tackle can be used to good effect when rock fishing for bass over very 'graunchy' ground with a gentle run of tide. Under these circumstances crab baits will outfish the worm and shellfish baits, because this is the type of location where large solitary bass are nosing around the weed-covered rocks expecting to locate their favourite food which I am certain is a juicy peeler or softback crab. For mounting peeler and softbacked crabs whole, I find that fine wired hooks with very small spade ends are the best. I mount the hooks on the nylon monofil hook snood with the spade end knot and tie a very small freshwater swivel to the end of it. Then I attach a baiting needle to the swivel and run this straight through the crab from just underneath the apron through its body so that it emerges approximately between its eye sockets. This effectively kills the crab and also allows me to pull the hook snood through the body, followed by the hook shank, so that the whole crab is now mounted neatly on the long shanked hook. The hook spade just protrudes from the front of the crab and the hook bend and point emerge under the crab's apron. For extra security, if the crabs are somewhat 'tender', I give the whole affair a couple of wraps with elasticated thread which is coloured either dark green or brown, taking the thread around the bend of the hook across the body of the crab and round the spade end of the hook.

Bigger crab portions can be mounted by the same method. The crabs need to be cut in half fore and aft across the shell and the baiting needle pushed through the leg sockets after the legs have been pulled off. Don't throw the legs away. They are used hooked onto the bend of the hook to help the crab body sit on the hook more securely and make it withstand the force of the cast. Again, a few turns of elasticated thread will make a secure bait that will stand up to both the cast and the motion of the waves.

173

This light surfcasting tackle set-up is ideal for float fishing from a variety of shorefishing locations. The strong casting shock leader can be dispensed with and the heavy leads are no longer necessary, and a level line can be used with a uniform breaking strain. The best design of floats I have ever seen and used are those originally intended for freshwater pike fishing. They are long and cigar-shaped with a very small hole down the centre from end to end, and they can be bought in various sizes. In shallow water which is less in depth than the length of the rod being used, they can be fished in a fixed position by passing the reel line through the central tunnel and securing the float with a small wooden plug top and bottom, or a couple of plastic leger stops. For deep water, to enable long casts to be made, the float needs to be used as a 'slider'. The float is stopped from slipping down onto the baited hook by fixing a swivel or a leger stop to the line and then securing a small piece of rubber band or a soft nylon brush bristle (either of which will pass easily through the rod rings) onto the line at the depth at which the tackle should present the suspended bait.

A very efficient method of checking the float at the correct fishing position is to use a sliding nylon 'stop knot'. To do this correctly, take a 6in length of 6–10lb line and fold it over itself to make a loop with equal lengths. Lay this loop along the reel line, and take one of the ends and put four turns around both the reel line and the other end of the looped nylon. Then pass the end of the line with which you have made the turns through the loop and gently tighten both loose ends after moistening them well with saliva or water. Do not overtighten, but tension the knot just sufficiently so that it will slide along the line without too much pressure being exerted. So that the sliding stop knot can pass easily through the rod rings, trim the ends off to leave them about an inch long. Incidentally, if a very heavy float is being used which moves the stop knot during fishing, refrain from tightening the stop knot too much or it will not slide freely along the line when adjustments need to be made. Merely tie another identical stop knot and place the two together on the line; one will act as a 'buffer lock' for the other and the problem will be solved.

This float-fishing technique is particularly effective for catching bass and pollack which forage around in deepwater gullies, and wrasse which are often to be taken from deepwater rock marks where the fish are often right under the feet of the angler as he stands on the rock ledges to cast his tackle. I favour live baits for this type of float fishing, especially large live prawns which are impaled on a fine wired hook by passing the point up through the third tail segment. Sandeels fished live are also a fine bait which will take a variety of fish: bass, pollack and coalfish from the rocks, and thornback rays, cod and all the flatfishes over sandy ground when fished on the bottom.

Piers, jetties and harbour walls respond very well to float fishing, particularly where there is a good depth of water around weed- and barnacle-encrusted piles. During the day, in full sunlight, if the water is clear and unclouded and there is lots of holidaymaker activity on the pier or harbour wall, very few fish will be taken except the odd 'strap' conger and a few suicidal dabs and flounders which hang themselves onto any type of tackle fished on the bottom. Around dusk, however, and once it is fully dark, an amazing transformation takes place at these raised fishing platforms.

Big bass, especially, come nosing around and are attracted by the downward shining lights. Large conger investigate the upper levels of the water. Deepwater species, under cover of darkness, lose their caution and swim inshore to investigate the possibilities of a feeding spree, particularly in harbours where commercial fishing boats often gut the last of the trawl-caught catch and dump the fish offal overboard close alongside the harbour wall.

If the pier lights are quite bright, float fishing can be done right under them without any added illumination being provided by the angler. For unlit piers and jetties, the new range of isotope freshwater floats are excellent. They open up a whole new world of after-dark float fishing hitherto untapped by anglers, who, before the advent of these new floats, had either to pack up and go home when darkness fell or provide something in the nature of electric headlamp illumination.

Some of the finest all-action sport can be obtained from the shore where there is a good depth of water close in, if spinning tackle is employed. At a pinch, the rod and reel used for light surfcasting can be pressed into service. In fact, I am sure that the added length of a 12ft bass rod, capable of throwing weighted lures a great distance, is superior to the general 8 or 9ft traditional purpose-built spinning rod, as those extra few feet of the beachcaster are a great asset for lifting fish clear of the rocks and also guiding them around snags such as pier ironwork uprights and horizontal underwater planks and girders.

Self-weighted lures, spinners and spoons are by far the best, as any added weights mounted along the line between the lure and the rod tip seem to destroy its action. To prevent kinking of the reel line, a really efficient, high-quality swivel should be incorporated into the terminal rig. I find a split-link swivel quite adequate, tied to the end of the reel line so that a succession of lures can be interchanged very quickly.

The predatory shore-caught species—mackerel, bass, pollack, coalfish and garfish—are the ones to expect on spinning tackle. To be effective, the water conditions for spinning must be clear so that the fish are feeding by sight rather than hunting down their food in cloudy water by smell. Where there are deepwater drop-offs around rocky headlands with a very powerful run of tide, a novel form of float spinning can be practised. Any small sea or freshwater float will do, provided it just supports the weight of the spinner or lure. With this method the spinner or lure can be fished or operated at any given depth. Float spinning is particularly useful therefore where the bottom is very snaggy.

To get the best results, set the spinner at a sufficient depth below the float so that it just clears the underwater rocks or weed. Then allow the float-suspended spinner or lure to be carried away on the current until it is a good distance from the fishing stance. By judiciously manipulating the rod tip and reeling in the line, the underwater lure can be made to perform all kinds of attractive marine antics. It can also be held stationary, supported by the float in the fastest of tidal runs without either sinking to the bottom and becoming snagged, or rising too high in the water almost to the surface. Strenuous casting is completely obviated with this float spinner method. When the tackle has been retrieved to a close-in position, it can then be released from the reel and allowed to sail off way downtide again so that a further fish-attracting retrieve can be started.

By far the widest known and most deadly spinning technique for saltwater fishing is what is known as 'the baited spoon' method for flounders and plaice. The spoons are either shiny metal or white plastic and they are mounted on a swivelled trace so that the revolving spoon precedes the bait at a distance of a few inches. As mentioned in the previous chapter, plaice and flounders are intensely curious fish which will follow a moving bait over the bottom and even rise up in the water to chase and intercept it. The baited spoon is cast out on a lightly leaded tackle and then retrieved in a series of jerks so that the spoon flutters over the sandy bottom and then dives down to produce puffs of sand which greatly interest the fish.

A variety of baits can be used on the trailing hook. Worms are considered best, either ragworms or small lugworms. These are not the only baits which are effective, however. It pays to experiment with all kinds of hook offerings; small pieces of razorfish, cockles and mussels will all take fish. At one time I did a series of experiments with baited flounder spoons and took some very good fish in a sandy and muddy bottomed harbour on ordinary garden worms made up into a cocktail with red maggots from a coarse fishing outing.

The tackle for both spinning and baited spoon fishing can be alternated between traditional light surfcasting gear and coarse fishing tackle. For heavy spinning, I use a 1–3oz bass rod with either a small multiplier or a fixed-spool reel. Stepping the power down a little, I favour an 11ft carp rod and a freshwater fixed-spool reel with three or four spools of line around the 6–12lb mark. For the very lightest of gear to be employed in harbours and sea lagoons, I call into service any of my coarse fishing rods that are suitable, from light 9ft spinning rods, intended originally for pike and perch, to swing tip and swimfeeder rods designed for use with lines around the 4–6lb mark.

The general rules for spinning are as follows. Clear water with a bright sunny sky: dull spoons in copper and brass. Bad lighting, or cloudy water: the most flashy spoons obtainable. The less visibility there is underwater, the more the fish will need to home in on artificial baits that transmit strong, fluttering vibrations into the water. Some new plastic sandeels have just appeared on the tackle scene which are self-weighted. The fish-attracting action of these very pliable, soft-bodied lures is nothing short of fantastic. When all else fails, give them a trial.

To round off this lengthy chapter on the subject of methods, rigs and baits for the various species of the shorecaster's quarry, I feel it important that the popular and recently increasing trend towards light tackle mullet fishing is thoroughly dealt with. The only way to approach mullet fishing successfully is to begin by clearing completely from your mind any preconceived ideas you have about what their behaviour patterns should be. The mullet is one fish which breaks all the rules and makes a set of its own every time you fish for it. The best way to come to terms with such an enigmatic fish is first to locate a shoal either in the sea, up a river or estuary, in a harbour or cruising up a creek, then study them for a few tidal sequences to see how they behave. You will soon have a fair idea of where they are and what they are doing at different states of the tidal flows. But for goodness sake do not for one moment imagine you have established how all mullet behave everywhere. What you have done is merely observed and noted the habits of one localised shoal. A mile or two up the river or in another harbour a short distance away, another shoal of fish will most probably react to tide, wind and weather in a completely different fashion.

I am of the opinion that mullet in the open sea are rather different fish in their behaviour patterns from mullet which run up rivers and creeks, or into harbours and boat marinas. Off the

Cornish coast, particularly at Porthcurno, I have observed large concentrated shoals of mullet being attracted shorewards by vast quantities of 'browse' groundbait being scattered over the surface of the water. The highly pungent 'browse', which is a revolting, brown, evil-smelling mixture of mashed-up pilchards (some of which smell to be at least 100 years old), bran, other secret ingredients and fish oil, is ladled into the sea from buckets with a kind of tin-lid-nailed-to-a-stick soup dispenser. There are even long established 'browse holes' in the rocks where over the years groundbait has been pulped to the right consistency and aroma. Under these open sea mullet fishing conditions, the tackle can be somewhat heavier than that employed in up-river and harbour locations. Light beachcasting gear can be used with 10lb line and a fairly small sea-fishing float and a fine wired short-shanked coarse-fishing hook about size 8. Where the water surface is broken or 'boily' around rocks, and float fishing is impracticable, a paternoster rig is the most suitable one to employ. In these rather strong water locations the mullet fisher's favourite standby bait of bread will not stay on the hook long enough; small harbour ragworms and tiny pieces of fish strip make a much more durable bait.

Once mullet come into what I will choose to term 'inland' waters, their caution seems to be sharpened according to the locations where they swim. Up rivers and in shallow creeks they are apt to be very susceptible to bankside noise and commotion and especially to the vibrations and shadows of walkers. In harbours, where food is plentiful, the attractions of unlimited nourishment seem to deaden or lull their senses a little and they accept noise and bustle as a part of this 'free feeding' environment.

This is where the coarse fisherman will be in his element. I use exclusively a 14½ft match rod, 3 or 4lb line on a large drummed 'Leeds' centre-pin reel, coarse fishing floats, split shot and all sizes of fine-wired, short-shanked, spade-end hooks from about size 8 down to a diminutive size 16, according to the bait I am using and my method of presentation of the tackle to the fish.

Long-trotting is my favourite method, and I sit myself down where a gentle tide run will carry my tackle up or downstream if in a river, or along the current line in a harbour or marina. Well dampened, mashed bread is a universal mullet groundbait, but see that it does not float; otherwise in such a marine location, flocks of hungry gulls will soon descend on your groundbait trail and quickly gulp it all down their hungry throats.

When the mullet are on the surface, a free-lined technique can be employed with just a hook loaded with floating crust and the line near the hook greased to make it float. This is a good method when the fish are very close to the angler's fishing position. When they are further away, a water-loaded bubble float can be used to good effect. This gives casting weight without it being clearly visible on the surface. To obtain a slow-sinking breadbait effect, when fishing at distance, load the bubble float with water until it just sinks very slowly through the water taking the bread-loaded hook down slowly with it.

If you can get your groundbait to sink at the same speed as your hookbait, then your chances of fooling the mullet are very high. For this long casting tackle technique, I swap over from a centre-pin reel to a coarse fishing fixed-spool reel loaded to within an eighth of an inch of the spool lip with line to facilitate easy casting.

12
Shore Lore, Night Fishing
and Safety Precautions

Throughout this book I have attempted to fire with enthusiasm for shorecasting a whole host of readers from all walks of life, both young and old. I therefore feel it my duty in this closing chapter to pass on everything I have learned on the subject of self-preservation so that those who have taken my advice will not only catch goodly bags of fish but will also continue to do so to a ripe old age, without any serious accidents marring their angling career.

Before me as I write, I have one of the weekly angling newspapers. It is dated late in October and in large black headlines on one page I read 'SORROW SUNDAY', followed by a report of the deaths of half a dozen men and a six-year-old boy — all anglers. Five of the deaths occurred because boating anglers disregarded local advice regarding safety and weather conditions. The most tragic happening took place when a father and his small son tried to fish from the end of a prohibited breakwater in a gale and were washed off it by mountainous seas.

Whenever I listen to the weather forecast on the radio and hear the announcement 'Attention all shipping — here is a gale warning', I feel very strongly that the opening phrase should be 'Attention all shipping and especially all sea anglers'. Generally, angling pleasureboaters are very weather conscious, except for a lunatic fringe who are abysmally ignorant of the devastating power of the sea. But, because shore fishermen operate from a location which is regarded as safe ground, they are apt to become careless and take chances which are sometimes fatal.

Before any angler, bait digger or casual shore walker sets foot near the tideline anywhere around our coastline, even on a fine, clear sunny day, he should be in possession of certain information which could save his life. First and foremost – and of the most vital importance – he must be aware of the tidal timings, not just some vague information such as 'The tide is going out' or 'It will be high tide soon'. What he needs to know is the exact timings of the tides, whether they are springs or neaps, and how far up the shoreline they will come.

I spend a great deal of time, especially during the summer months, around the Flamborough Head area on the Yorkshire coast. From where I am sitting now at my desk writing these lines in the middle of winter, I can safely forecast with the utmost certainty that this area will, during the holiday months of next summer, claim at least three or four people dead and many more – perhaps a dozen or so – rescued by coastguards, rock climbing experts, lifeboats or commercial fishermen after a very narrow escape. 'What happens?' you may ask. 'Why is the area so dangerous?' To give a good comparison, I would reply that it is no more dangerous than a pedestrian zebra crossing. Provided you do not dash across at red into the stream of traffic, you are safe. If, however, you foolishly choose to disregard the colour of the lights, you are instantly courting disaster and may end up battered on the road.

It is just the same around Flamborough Head. Lots of holiday-makers disregard local warnings telling them that to attempt to walk around the Head along the beach at low tide is dangerous. They see a gleaming, sunlit, tide-washed beach with the water leaving a clear margin along the undercliff and they set off, usually with not the slightest idea of whether the tide is going in or out. Somewhere along the way, they find that they have to climb a little here and there to reach the next piece of beach. Eventually, they climb around a rocky point and find their way barred by a steep overhang which cannot be negotiated. Turning back, after scrambling around for a while, they then discover their retreat is cut off by the rising tide. Now they are in real trouble and at this point they panic and attempt to climb upward to make good their escape to the cliff top. Eventually they either find a perch high up on the cliff face from which they cannot move, and scream for help, or they fall to their deaths onto the rocks below, or they are trapped under an overhang and drowned by the advancing tide. A senseless waste of precious lives, yet every year without fail the fatalities appear in the press and are announced on the radio and television.

Please do not ignore local advice and warnings. They are given in good faith by people intimately acquainted with the dangers that are ever present in certain areas. They have no wish to spoil your enjoyment. Their only desire is for you to visit their stretch of the coastline, enjoy it, and remain safe while you are doing so.

In complete contrast to rocky areas with towering cliffs, which by their very appearance would seem to suggest hidden dangers, very flat shorelines can often prove most deceptively hazardous. Beach fishermen are always on the lookout for natural 'holes' along the shore, where the run of the tide or a recent storm has gouged a deep channel or trough in the sand or shingle. These places which give a greater depth of water when covered by the tide are renowned for their ability to produce good bags of fish (especially winter cod) as they act as a natural larder for the fish. Small marine animals and bait-size fish are attracted to them, especially if the bottom is uneven and stony and the water surface above them is not so rough due to the added water depth. What usually happens at such locations is that the shore angler carefully notes the position of these deepwater gullies and decides to fish them on the next series of big spring tides. Perhaps there is a long trough which dries out at half tide down, then a flat sandbank some distance further down the shoreline, followed by a deepwater low tide hole which is only reached with a long cast at the very bottom of a big tide which recedes very far down the beach.

As the tide gradually recedes, the eager shore angler follows it down the beach across the gullies and right down to the very bottom of the littoral zone, wading across the gullies as they slowly dry out so that he eventually is able to cast into the 'bottom-of-tide' deepwater hole and really get among the fish. When the fishing is exceptionally good, the angler is apt to be caught off his guard when the tide starts to rise again. He lingers for just one more cast, and then finds to his horror that a great deep lagoon of water has craftily sneaked up behind him and he is unfortunately marooned on his little patch of high ground.

With a red face, I freely admit to having this happen to me a time or two, but luckily I have managed to extricate myself without losing my life and all my tackle as well. This danger of being cut off by the rising tide is particularly applicable at night in the dark. The angler has no idea of how fast the tide is rising behind him as he cannot see how far it has crept up the shoreline. In such a dodgy situation, my advice is to choose a less dangerous part of the shoreline, especially for night fishing, and stay alive.

The cardinal rule for shore fishing after dark is, do not go alone if humanly possible, and be completely conversant with every detail of the terrain you will fish and walk over. To reinforce these statements, let us consider the safety aspects purely from a visibility point of view.

During the daytime, anyone in trouble on a beach, rocks or cliffs is liable to be spotted by someone with a pair of binoculars who will alert the local rescue service to get him out of his predicament. At night the whole scene is blacked out. Whilst boaters carry flares to attract attention to themselves, I have yet to hear of a shore angler who takes this safety precaution. Therefore be self-reliant and always try very hard to keep yourself out of trouble. Because if you don't, there is the distinct possibility that there will be no one to see what a fix you are in and get you out of it.

From a personal safety point of view, there are two distinct kinds of night fishing, quite different from each other. On well-lit piers, jetties and harbour walls, where lots of anglers are congregated, anyone getting into difficulties has help within easy shouting distance. To a lesser extent this is so on a beach where a whole line of anglers are fishing together. It is when you strike out on your own to fish remote shorelines that the self-preservation aspect must be carefully considered.

So far as equipment is concerned, you must ensure that you have adequate lighting facilities both for your fish catching and to enable you to proceed to and from your fishing mark in safety. As an extra precaution against being caught out half way down a steep rock-mark path with a broken paraffin pressure lantern that has suddenly plunged you into complete darkness, some form of standby lighting is necessary, preferably of the electric battery-powered kind. Never rely totally on just one light source. You may approach a tricky rock mark just before dark and get safely onto it, only to find that the powerful electric headlamp which was to be your sole illumination on your after-dark journey back to safe ground will not work. Somehow the raised switch has been pushed into the 'on' position in your tackle bag and the batteries are flat. Always carry a spare set of batteries and a replacement bulb, and to obviate the possibility of an electric headlamp getting its power pack switch moved into the 'on' position while it is in your tackle bag or haversack, tape the switch firmly in the 'off' position with a piece of sticky plaster.

I do not like to climb down steep rocks carrying a lighted paraffin pressure lamp as a source of illumination, especially if I am in an angling group. If the lamp man slips and drops the light, it could stove someone's skull in or shower them with red hot glass, not to mention leaving all the rock scaling party in total darkness. Far better if every climber is fitted with his own electric headlight, making each member of the party totally self-sufficient.

A word here on creature comforts for night anglers. When planning an all-night trip it is essential to bear in mind that night temperatures on open shorelines drop far below those in the daytime. Keen overnight frosts usually take place in the early morning hours, which coincide with the period when the human body is at its lowest ebb and liable to feel the cold more than at any other time. With this precise aspect of the warmth problem in mind, the sensible angler must make sure that he has available all the necessary clothing to keep him warm and dry. Also some form of portable shelter (a 'Brolly-Camp' or a large umbrella with a canvas windbreaker) behind which he can shelter to avoid the rapid body-chilling effect of being constantly buffeted by a freezing wind, which not only lowers the temperature but the angler's morale as well.

Arrangements for portable shelters can, of course, only be made on steep-to beaches where the tides does not run right up the shoreline. For flat beaches, where the angler has to be constantly on the move either up or down following the tide in or out, he must face the rather chilling fact that he will be standing or sitting completely exposed to the elements all the time he is fishing. The most sensible way to approach this kind of situation is to fish in three- or four-hour stints with an above tide level base-camp situated well up the shoreline, to which the fisherman can retire for a rest period and a warming-up session at the desired times.

Rock-mark fishing at night is fraught with danger. Not so much if the fishing position is a huge, flat rocky table over which the tide will not rise; these are reasonably safe. The rock angling I have in mind is the fairly flat, lumpy shoreline with boulders, deep gullies and an assortment of small rock tables over which the tide ebbs and flows. These marks are always tricky, even in daylight, as the angler is frequently unable to see exactly how high the tide has risen behind him due to rocky projections blocking off his vision on the shoreward side. After witnessing quite a number of angling accidents (with a few very sobering fatalities), I am now inclined to be a cautious fisherman and put a sensible taboo on suicidal rock marks after dark.

Here on the Yorkshire coast, we have what is known as a cliff erosion problem which causes some very dangerous situations for anglers. In winter, after high tides and heavy rain, certain parts of the cliffs become very soft and sploshy, but these soft patches are not always apparent, especially in the dark. It is essential when going down the cliffs in daylight to note well a suitable line of retreat for your return journey in the dark. A series of white painted sticks placed here and there are very helpful when you make your return scramble after dark. I have lost a couple of pairs of waders myself when I have become slightly stuck and managed to drag myself clear and scramble to the cliff top, completely covered in mud and scared out of my wits by the unnerving experience.

On one occasion, I assisted in an 'angler stuck in the mud' rescue and I have never forgotten it. The poor soul was discovered just as dawn was breaking on a muddy cliff up to his armpits in the ooze and more dead than alive, after having been there in the freezing cold half the night shouting his head off for help. With the aid of four long ladders, several planks and a stout rope, he was finally drawn, with a plop like a champagne cork, from the mud. He needed hospital treatment for shock and exposure and never went down a muddy cliff again, having been thoroughly scared by the harrowing thought that if help did not arrive he would eventually be sucked beneath the surface of the mud and entombed in it.

One other danger of eroded cliffs is the chance of a large section falling on to an angler who is standing below. We had such a tragedy about four years ago. A young girl who was accompanying her father on a beach fishing trip was sheltering beneath an overhang during a violent shower of rain. Suddenly a great piece slipped and completely covered her; she was dead by the time a rescue squad had finished digging her out of the sticky mess.

There are some golden rules for keeping out of trouble, when venturing out over mudflats to dig bait or to fish. Make sure that the mud you are walking on has a firm surface underneath it. If the mud comes past your ankles and even up to your calves you can manage to walk over it in thigh boots. However, once you begin to sink past the level of your calves, watch out for trouble. The deeper each foot sinks, the higher you must raise the other one in order to take a step. Eventually, one foot will be sunk deeply into the mud and as you try to heave it clear, to make a forward movement, you will overbalance with the effort of extricating it and land flat on your back in the ooze. When this happens, the floppy tops of your thigh boots rapidly fill with mud as you struggle and they become very weighty, thereby further hampering your chances of regaining an upright position. If no one is at hand to assist you to get upright again, you are in a dangerous fix. The only thing to do to get out of your horizontal mudbath is to rid yourself of the thigh boots and do a swimming motion to a section of firmer ground where you can get your feet underneath yourself again.

When venturing out on mud which has a firm surface underneath it, always take along your monopod and probe the ground before you as you proceed. This will ensure that you have a firm footing before you move forward and prevent you suddenly floundering into an unforeseen mud hole.

There are quite a few pitfalls to avoid when bait digging and crab hunting, apart from being lost in a sudden mist or fog or being cut off by the rising tide. Some anglers, when digging lugworms over a very wet, muddy shoreline, carelessly allow one foot to remain in the digging hole as they work with the broad-tined 'spud' fork. This is the height of folly. The foot in the 'diggings' eventually becomes covered with mud and water and is out of sight. When that happens watch out! You could plunge your fork in to extract another monster worm and find you have impaled your own foot.

The extraction of peeler and soft crabs from rock holes and cracks is dangerous, if you do it with your bare hands instead of an old blunt gaff or a 'crab hook' made up from heavy gauge wire or thin mild steel rod bent to the appropriate shape. When working right down on the bottom section of the littoral zone, quite a number of finger-'noshing' live creatures may be encountered. The most dangerous could be a conger eel which would not take kindly to having its eye poked sharply with a human finger. It could retaliate by clamping its crushing jaws on to the offending member and firmly tethering the luckless angler to await the awful doom of a trapped hand and a rising tide. Big edible crabs can also do a painful crushing job on your hand, if you plunge it into a hole where they are tightly ensconced and they flex their back legs and front claws to crush your hand up against the top of the tunnel in which they are hiding.

I have a motley collection of five fishing coats, all in varying stages of disrepair, and collectively they give off a shocking fish-dock aroma. However, in the pockets of each one, somewhere tucked away safely, is a cheap compass with a luminous dial. All shoreline wanderers and bait diggers should regard a pocket compass as an essential lifesaving insurance. On a rising tide, if you are way out on a remote shoreline with deep gullies between you and safe high ground and a thick mist or fog descends suddenly, your chances of getting back to safety with the minimum delay are nil without that vital piece of direction-finding equipment. But do remember to check your directions with it before you set off out across the mud or sand. Your compass is useless if you have no idea of the bearing to walk back on. It is also much more than useless if you have left it at home!

It is very exhilarating and also attractively dangerous to fish from high rock or cliff marks and off rocky headlands. But two types of accident can happen to the adventurous souls who try it. In wet weather the descending grass tracks can become like a slippery water chute, so that even if you are wearing studded climbing boots your progress down can suddenly become like a human toboggan ride rather than a controlled climb. In such circumstances, if your fishing position, which you are climbing down to, is a narrow ledge with a sheer drop below it, you could, whilst doing an uncontrolled slide down the slippery grass track, overshoot your mark and be unable to stop.

Exposed rock marks on 'Heads' and promontories which project seawards are also death traps when a heavy groundswell is running and freak 'rogue' waves or sudden surges take place. These rare enormous waves are a carry-over from violent storms way out in the ocean. The weather conditions when such happenings take place are very often completely misleading. The day may be unusually still, warm and sunny with a long, apparently lazy, and seemingly perfectly safe swell on the water. Ideal fishing conditions you may think; but nothing could be further from the truth. At irregular intervals and completely without prior indication, a sudden terrifying wall of water will rise up and sweep over everything. Then the sea once more settles down again to its normal wave pattern.

There are no sensible precautions that an angler can take when such unusual wave conditions prevail, other than to keep clear of such rock marks altogether until the groundswell has subsided. Keeping a careful watch for big waves while you are perched on a rocky ledge fishing is not the answer. If your retreat is up a slippery, precipitous climb which takes a few minutes to get you away from the danger zone, you can be assured that the wave will not delay its inward sweep until you are out of its reach. If in doubt about the personal safety aspect of a fishing mark *keep off it altogether* and stay alive.

The fish you catch can often be highly dangerous if you do not recognise what they are, or don't know how to deal with them properly – either to unhook and return them, or to despatch them in a quick and humane manner if they are to be eaten. We have already considered that truly lethal pest the weever fish elsewhere, so I will not describe it in detail again, but merely issue an additional warning to avoid contact with it.

Quite a number of nasty happenings take place when an angler is bringing a fish in through the waves, and his companion gleefully plunges his hands into the surf to grab it before he knows what exactly is on the end of the line. Thornback rays have very sharp spines on the ends of their tails (a favourite grabbing place) and also on their wings, which can badly lacerate an unwary hand. Sting rays have a whiplash tail equipped with a spike which is capable of inflicting serious injuries and even slicing through rubber boots – definitely not a fish to grope around for in the dark in order to help your angling partner to land his catch. If in doubt about the nature of the species of fish being caught, keep well away from it until it is hauled, by the man with the rod, onto dry land and then you can examine it at your leisure and decide how best to deal with it.

The best and safest way to deal with any dangerous species is to cut the hook snood as near to the fish as possible and release it back into its natural element. Bigger fish, if to be retained for the table, should be killed immediately they are landed and not left to gasp out their lives painfully out of water. Either give them a heavy blow just behind the eyes with a big stone or completely sever their spinal cord behind the head with a strong, sharp bladed knife of the rigid pattern, not a folding knife which may close up on your fingers if the fish kicks.

Never try to unhook a large live fish with dangerous teeth if you don't know how to deal with it properly, or if you are not in possession of a special sea angler's 'hook out' disgorger. Far better, if you are returning it, to cut the trace and put the fish back than risk a few badly crunched fingers. Conger eels are particularly dangerous, as they often appear to be dead when in fact they are very much alive and quite capable of doing great damage if anyone should molest them.

My last warning before I say farewell and good fishing is on that controversial subject of long casting and the danger it can cause if certain very anti-social casting styles are performed on crowded beaches. It is my personal belief that the 250yd casting mark which has now been exceeded on the tournament field is what I shall choose to call a suicide distance, when viewed in terms of practical fishing performance. Please don't let the casting experts brainwash you into believing that extreme distance and safety go hand in hand. At a recent surfcasting tournament one 'star' lead slinger 'cracked-off' seven times in a total of twelve casts. Translated into an angling performance on a fishing beach, that is seven flying leads in orbit to places unknown. Apart from the loss of fishing time and the cost of all those lost terminal tackles, how about anyone innocently standing in the 'fall-out' zone and having the chance of getting his brains bashed in—seven times? If such 'tournament tactics' ever become commonplace on our shorelines it will be necessary—in the interests of staying alive—for anglers to discard their 'arctic suits' and 'fur trappers' headgear and replace them with bullet-proof vests and crash helmets.

191

Index